Teashops around Bristol and Bath

Nigel Vile

COUNTRYSIDE BOOKS
NEWBURY, BERKSHIRE

First published 2002
© Nigel Vile 2002

COUNTRYSIDE BOOKS
3 Catherine Road
Newbury, Berkshire

To view our complete range of books,
please visit us at
www.countrysidebooks.co.uk

ISBN 1 85306 733 4

Designed by Graham Whiteman
Cover illustration by Colin Doggett
Photographs and maps by the author

Produced through MRM Associates Ltd., Reading
Printed by J. W. Arrowsmith Ltd., Bristol

Contents

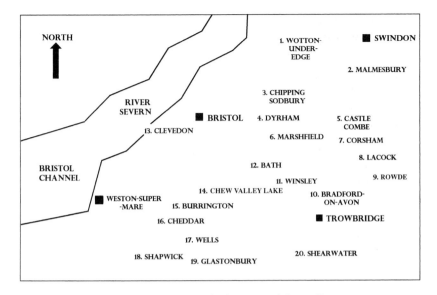

Map labels:

NORTH

1. WOTTON-UNDER-EDGE

■ SWINDON

2. MALMESBURY

3. CHIPPING SODBURY

RIVER SEVERN

■ BRISTOL

4. DYRHAM

5. CASTLE COMBE

13. CLEVEDON

6. MARSHFIELD

7. CORSHAM

8. LACOCK

BRISTOL CHANNEL

12. BATH

11. WINSLEY

9. ROWDE

14. CHEW VALLEY LAKE

10. BRADFORD-ON-AVON

■ WESTON-SUPER-MARE

15. BURRINGTON

■ TROWBRIDGE

16. CHEDDAR

17. WELLS

18. SHAPWICK

19. GLASTONBURY

20. SHEARWATER

Area map showing the location of the walks.

19 Glastonbury and the Tor *(4 miles)*   89
    A chance to explore the mystical and magical landscape in and
    around Glastonbury, with its Tor the literal highpoint of the
    walk.

20 Shearwater and Longbridge Deverill *(5 miles)*   93
    Woodland paths in the vicinity of this beautiful lake, hidden in
    a quiet corner of the Longleat Estate.

Introduction

The countryside around Bath and Bristol offers a fine natural setting for each of the walks included in this book. This is an area with a tremendously rich and varied landscape. To the west lie the Severn Estuary and the Bristol Channel, a unique environment of mudflats and estuarine wildlife. Northwards are the Cotswold Hills, where numerous stone villages have launched any number of picture postcards and calendars. To the south of Bristol and Bath lie the Mendip Hills, a vast area of limestone upland, dissected and riddled by gorges and potholes. Overshadowed by the Mendip Hills are the Somerset Levels, one of the most important wetland habitats in the country.

If all that were not enough, there is even more! Head east from Bath and Bristol and the pastoral landscape of Wiltshire with its chalk hills opens up. Red-brick and thatch cottages begin to predominate, as the golden limestone found further west is gradually replaced by clay as a building material. Finally, there is the common thread that links Bristol, Bath and the towns beyond — the River Avon and its associated artificial companion the Kennet and Avon Canal. The river bank and canal towpath provide some of the most attractive and popular walking in the region.

Each of these diverse and fascinating landscape types is explored in this book. At Castle Combe, for example, we discover all that is best about Cotswold villages, whilst at Clevedon there is the opportunity to stroll along the Bristol Channel coast. Head south to Shapwick and Burrington, and there are walks that quite literally cover the highs and lows of walking in Somerset. The lowland heath at Shapwick could not present more of a contrast compared with the upland moors above Burrington. At Corsham, there is the chance to explore one of Wiltshire's great landed estates, whilst one of the most mystical centres in Europe is the focus of the walk at Glastonbury. If variety is the spice of life, then walkers fortunate enough to live in the Bath and Bristol area are truly blessed!

The twenty routes featured in this collection are each centred upon a teashop or café, perhaps at journey's end or otherwise at some convenient point along the way. The range of teashops is as rich and varied as the range of landscape types, too. In Bath, for example, there is the opportunity to visit Sally Lunn's, located in the oldest house in this most historic of cities, whilst at Bradford-on-Avon, your cream tea or morning coffee can be enjoyed in a former lengthman's cottage alongside the Kennet and Avon Canal. By way of complete contrast, the café at Shapwick in the heart of the Somerset Levels is situated in a garden centre, whilst the tearoom at Winsley is located in a large chalet-style garden shed. At Clevedon, we find a traditional seafront café, whilst at Burrington 'the cup that cheers but does not inebriate' — to quote William Cowper — is actually served in licensed premises!

Most of the tearooms in this book are open during normal business hours, usually seven days a week in the holiday season. At off-peak times, the hours can be a little more random. With this in mind, I have provided the telephone number of each café and tearoom should you wish to make a precise enquiry prior to setting off on one of the walks. To give you a flavour of what to expect, a brief pen portrait of each refreshment stop is provided. As well as a few words about the history and character of each café or teashop, there is a description of the refreshments on offer.

The walks are deliberately of modest length, making them suitable for all kinds of walkers, from the more mature person to the typical family group. Each should provide a morning or afternoon of exercise and interest, which can be accompanied by morning coffee, lunch or afternoon tea in a relaxing atmosphere. Whilst the directions and sketch maps in this book are adequate for route finding — compasses won't be needed in this part of the world — it is always a good idea for the walker to carry an OS map as well, if only to help with identifying the main features or views. The appropriate OS Landranger sheet, 1:50 000, is specified for each walk, as well as the relevant OS Explorer sheet on a scale of 1:25 000.

When visiting each tearoom or café, you could well be hot and sticky or damp and muddy. It is only polite therefore to both the proprietor and the other customers if you attempt some form of wash and brush-up before enjoying your teas and coffees. If nothing else, at least leave muddy boots outside somewhere. All of this should really go without saying but, in the past, some owners of pubs, cafés and tearooms have actively discouraged walkers from using their premises on account of the thoughtless actions of a minority of walkers... and authors of walking guidebooks have received unpleasant letters as a consequence!

Finally, it remains for me to wish you happy walking in this lovely region. Not only do these routes open up the countryside around two of Britain's greatest cities, they also introduce some of our best tearooms and cafés. Please remember, too, that although a traditional English cream tea is high on calories, you will have earned this small treat on account of the energy expended during the walk. I hope that this book will bring you many hours of pleasure.

Nigel Vile

7

Walk 1
WOTTON-UNDER-EDGE
and NIBLEY KNOLL

The Cotswold market town of Wotton-under-Edge enjoys a sheltered location nestling deep beneath the Cotswold escarpment. From Wotton's main street, this walk climbs steeply onto the hilltops above the town before following delightful woodland paths through Westridge Wood to the Tyndale Monument, high above North Nibley. The route returns along a short section of the Cotswold Way, with the grand finale being the quite exceptional view from Wotton Hill, a view which extends across much of South Gloucestershire towards the distant Welsh Hills.

Wotton Coffee Shop, part of a guesthouse, fronts onto the town's bustling High Street. Sitting on the Cotswold Way, this is one refreshment stop that must have been visited by quite literally thousands of walkers en route between Bath and Chipping Campden. Behind the shop is a delightful walled garden, which is just the spot to relax and linger on a warm summer's day. Morning coffee, light lunches and afternoon teas are all there to tempt the passing visitor, with the traditional English cream tea being a popular option. If your appetite demands something a little more filling, then one of the filled jacket potatoes — or even a portion of casserole — will surely appeal. Open during normal business hours, Monday to Saturday. Telephone: 01453 843158. As well as several pubs, Wotton-under-Edge also boasts the Cyber Fish Café. Located in the main street, this provides an alternative should the Wotton Coffee Shop be closed, and it is open daily, including Sunday afternoons.

DISTANCE: 4½ miles.
MAPS: OS Landranger 162 or Explorer 167.
STARTING POINT: The public car park at the rear of Wotton-under-Edge's High Street. This car park is clearly signposted as you approach the town centre (GR 756931).
HOW TO GET THERE: Wotton-under-Edge lies on the B4058 road that runs between Bristol and Nailsworth.

THE WALK

1. From the car park, walk through to the High Street. Turn right and, at the bottom of the High Street, turn left into Church Street. Continue along to the B4058 and the war memorial, before crossing over into Culverhay by Edbrook House. Continue along past St Mary the Virgin church, before turning left into Adeys Lane. Follow this lane uphill for ½ mile to a hilltop junction with another road — the Old London Road.

Wotton-under-Edge is an attractive market town, whose prosperity can be traced back to the heyday of the West of England cloth trade in the 17th and 18th centuries. Prior to this, the town had actually been burned to the ground by King John's mercenaries in the early 13th century because of the town's connection with the Berkeley family of nearby Berkeley Castle. This enabled Wotton to be rebuilt as a planned town, which was given borough status in 1253. Nestling beneath the Cotswold escarpment — hence the appendage 'Edge' — there are many fine buildings in the town. These include the 17th-century Perry's Almshouses in Church Street, as well as the imposing church of St Mary the Virgin, with its fine Perpendicular tower.

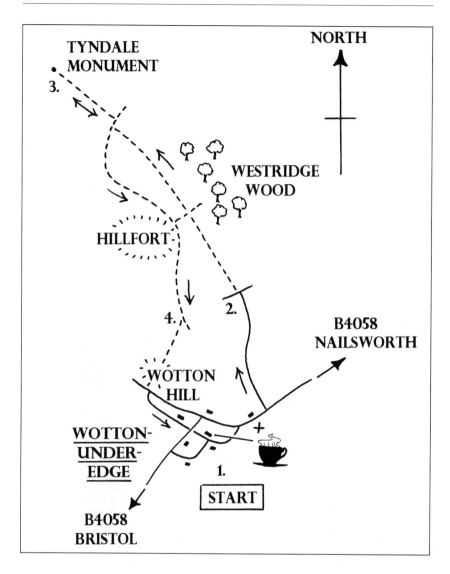

2. Turn left, then shortly right along an enclosed bridlepath. Follow this track ahead for 600 yards, ignoring right turns into the woodland along the way, until the track reaches a major junction. Cross straight over, and continue following the path into Westridge Wood. In 150 yards, ignore a right fork, keeping ahead instead for 200 yards to a prominent crosstrack. Cross this track, and follow the less well defined path ahead. In another 250 yards, paths come in on the right. Keep walking ahead for 100 yards until a main crosstrack is reached. Turn right and, almost immediately, fork left — there is a Cotswold Way sign. Pass through an area of beech trees before entering an open hilltop field. Follow the fence ahead as far as the Tyndale Monument.

The Tyndale Monument, sited high on Nibley Knoll, is a landmark for many miles around this quiet corner of South Gloucestershire. Erected in 1866, it commemorates the life and work of William Tyndale who translated the New Testament into English. He was later martyred at Vilorde in Flanders in 1536. Tradition maintains that Tyndale was born at North Nibley in 1494, a fact keenly disputed by the residents of Slimbridge, another Gloucestershire village. The monument is 26 feet square and 111 feet high, and its key can be obtained from the village of North Nibley... but this would involve descending and ascending the knoll twice! The view from below the monument looking across the Severn Estuary towards Wales is quite exceptional.

3. Retrace your steps across the hilltop field, and back through the area of beech trees to a junction. Turn right, and shortly you will reach the path on the left we followed earlier. Ignore this path, and continue onto a second path that forks off on the left, with a blue arrow marker on a

Wotton Hill

tree. Follow this path — the Cotswold Way — in a southerly direction for just over ½ mile, keeping directly ahead at a couple of crossings along the way, always with an eye out for the blue arrows. At a junction by a Cotswold Way marker post, ignore the left turn and keep directly ahead, an open field to the left. In ½ mile, the track bears left, whilst on the right is a National Trust 'Westridge Wood' sign.

Westridge Wood is an excellent example of typical Cotswold woodland, with beech and ash being the most common broad-leaved trees, and larch the most abundant conifer. Spring is certainly the best time of year to visit this fine woodland, when you will find carpets of dog's mercury, primroses and wood anemone along the way. Goldcrest and treecreeper can be numbered amongst the resident bird population, with both willow warbler and chiffchaff being seasonal visitors. Hidden deep in the woodland are Brackenbury Ditches, an Iron Age hillfort now almost totally obscured by tree cover. The path passes the widely spaced eastern banks and ditches, which face a mass of relatively flat land.

4. At this point, keep directly ahead into an open field. Follow the right-hand field boundary alongside the woodland to a kissing gate in the far right corner of the field. Beyond this gate, drop downhill to a clump of pine trees on Wotton Hill. Below these trees, follow the Cotswold Way as it enters some bushes before dropping downhill to a lane. Cross this lane, and continue following the path downhill to reach the B4060. Turn left, pass the Old London Road before taking the first right into Bradley Street. Follow this road for 300 yards to reach the B4058. Cross into Wotton's High Street, where the Wotton Coffee Shop is on the left-hand side. The first turning on the right is Market Street, which leads back to the car park.

Walk 2
MALMESBURY and the RIVER AVON

There is no doubting that Malmesbury is a town of great antiquity. As you approach the town, the signposts point out to all and sundry that this is 'England's Oldest Borough', a fact confirmed by the magnificent outline of the abbey that dominates the town's skyline. The actual Royal Charter conferring borough status was granted by Alfred the Great back in AD 880. The town itself sits upon a hilltop overlooking two branches of the River Avon, which meet here. This quite delightful town trail gives every opportunity to discover the historic heart of Malmesbury, as well as exploring the meadows that border the Avon on its fringes. Altogether, a marvellous excuse to visit one of England's finest small towns.

 Amanda's teashop fronts onto Oxford Street in the busy heart of Malmesbury. It is a perfect oasis of calm from the busy streets in and around the town centre, an ideal spot to rest and linger whilst enjoying morning coffee or afternoon tea, or perhaps one of the tempting light lunches on the menu. These might typically include an open bacon, sausage and tomato sandwich or a filled jacket potato. The various cakes and pastries on the menu — flapjacks, shortbread, fridge cake or Danish pastries, for example — will prove difficult to resist, as will the delightfully named 'Sybil's Sublime Tea'. Comprising scones, cream and jam, salmon and cucumber sandwiches, homemade cakes and a pot of tea, this archetypal English tea, if consumed at the end of the walk, will certainly restore all of those calories burned off along the way! Open during normal business hours, Monday to Saturday. Telephone: 01666 829356. There are many pubs and cafes in Malmesbury. Most conveniently located should Miranda's be closed is the Whole Hog by the Market Cross. Although technically a restaurant, the Whole Hog serves beers, soft drinks and coffees.

DISTANCE: 2 miles.

MAPS: OS Landranger 173 or Explorer 168.

STARTING POINT: The long-term Old Station car park below Malmesbury Abbey alongside the River Avon (GR 933875).

HOW TO GET THERE: The A429 Chippenham to Cirencester road bypasses the town of Malmesbury. Leave the A429 at its junction with the B4014 Tetbury road north of Malmesbury. Follow the Tetbury road for ½ mile before turning left to follow the signs to the long-term car park in Malmesbury. Incidentally, the long-term car park is clearly signposted from the A429.

THE WALK

History is everywhere in the town, with the ancient abbey being but the jewel in the crown. The market cross dating from 1490, almshouses dating from the 17th century and a former four-storey cloth mill also lie along the route. The mill reminds the visitor that Malmesbury was at one time a thriving weaving centre, with the River Avon powering the local waterwheels. Malmesbury marks the confluence of two of the river's tributaries — the River Avon (Tetbury Branch) and the River Avon (Sherston Branch). Both tributaries are followed along the way, their rural setting contrasting with the town section of the walk.

1. Walk to the end of the car park below the abbey. Rather than crossing the bridge over the Avon and following the path up to the abbey, turn left away from the river. Shortly, on the right, pass through a wooden handgate to enter the Conygre Mead Reserve. Follow the footpath by the river downstream to join the road by the Duke of York pub. Turn right, cross St Leonard's Bridge, turn left down some steps and cross a causeway

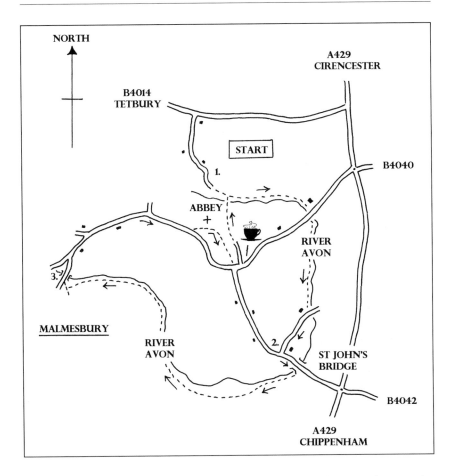

into the riverside meadow called Longmead. Cross this meadow to the far right corner, and pass below the abutments of the defunct Malmesbury Railway before entering the next meadow. Cross to the far left corner of this meadow, cross a bridge over the Avon and continue along the path alongside the local bowling green to a lane. Turn right, cross the Avon and continue along St John's Street to its junction with the High Street.

2. Cross the main road, turn left and almost immediately right through the park gates just before St John's Bridge. Immediately, turn left over the footbridge that runs parallel to the main road. Once across this footbridge, keep ahead for a few yards before passing through the handgate on the right into the meadows alongside the Avon. Follow the river across the first field to a handgate. Continue alongside the river in a second field for a short distance to a footbridge before entering the next field. Continue following the river until you reach a wooden handgate. In the next two fields, follow the hedgerow on the right, one field between the path and the Avon. In the far right corner of the second field, pass through a gap in the hedge into the next field, a stone clapper bridge on the right. Continue following the river upstream for 200 yards to reach a gate and stile, before following a track down to a lane.

3. Turn right, cross Turtle Bridge and follow the road around a sharp right bend up to Bristol Street. Turn right, and continue along Bristol Street to the Triangle. Turn right out of the Triangle along Abbey Row to reach the Old Bell Hotel. Enter the abbey churchyard just past the hotel and continue along to the entrance to the abbey. Turn right, follow the path down to the churchyard gate and the market cross. Turn left, pass in front of the Whole Hog Restaurant before turning left down the side turning that runs alongside the Whole Hog. (If you follow the main road ahead rather than turning left — Oxford Street — Amanda's teashop is a few yards along on the left-hand side.) Where this side turning ends, continue along the footpath past the Cloister Garden by the side of the abbey. Continue down the steps and across the Avon back to the car park.

Malmesbury from the River Avon

Walk 3
CHIPPING SODBURY, LITTLE SODBURY
and OLD SODBURY

Two distinct landscape types, the Severn Vale and the Cotswold escarpment, dominate South Gloucestershire. From the old market town of Chipping Sodbury, this walk heads across the eastern fringes of the Vale to visit the neighbouring villages of Little Sodbury and Old Sodbury. Set against what is colloquially known as the Cotswold Edge, the escarpment provides a grand backdrop throughout this ramble. One of the longer walks in this book, this really is the perfect introduction to the South Gloucestershire countryside.

The wide main street in Chipping Sodbury — appropriately enough known as 'Broad Street' — is clear evidence of the town's former status as a local market centre. It is lined by attractive properties, including a number of former coaching inns, and tucked in amongst them is the diminutive Poppy's Tea Rooms, its bright exterior, including a colourful sign and pretty hanging baskets, offering a welcoming feel. Depending on the time of day, customers can enjoy morning coffee, light lunches or cream teas, with a varied and interesting selection of cakes and pastries on offer. These include carrot cake and caramel slices, as well as Danish pastries and homemade shortbread. With its attractive décor, pine tables and chairs and wall prints, Poppy's is relaxing and friendly. Open during normal business hours, seven days a week. Telephone: 01454 313328.

DISTANCE: 6 miles.

MAPS: OS Landranger 172 or Explorer 167.

STARTING POINT: The public car park just off Wickwar Road in Chipping Sodbury (GR 727824).

HOW TO GET THERE: Chipping Sodbury lies on the A432, approximately 12 miles north-east of Bristol. Follow the main road into the town's main street, before turning onto the B4060 Wickwar Road. In 250 yards, just past the church, turn left into the signposted car park.

THE WALK

Chipping Sodbury was first established in the 12th century by William le Gros, Lord of the Manor of Sodbury. In 1218, Henry III granted William's grandson a charter for a market and fairs, and the grid system street plan was laid out, with its wide market street and the long burgage plots behind its houses. Burgage plots are plots of land a town retained for a yearly rental. The main street is full of fine old buildings that date back as far as the 16th century, stretching from the gabled 16th century Grapes Hotel at the western end of the main street to the Portcullis, a 17th century coaching inn that was once a meeting place for the Beaufort Hunt. In between are any number of old hostelries, with many archways, further reminders of the importance of Chipping Sodbury in the days of horse transport. The town was an important cloth centre until the 18th century, when the local cloth trade steadily declined. Being in a rich agricultural area, however, the town continued to thrive as a market centre, although today Chipping Sodbury is largely a base for commuting to Bristol.

1. Leave the car park, turn right along Wickwar Road and, in 40 yards, just before the church, turn left along a public footpath that borders a new housing development. This soon becomes a gravelled path, marked

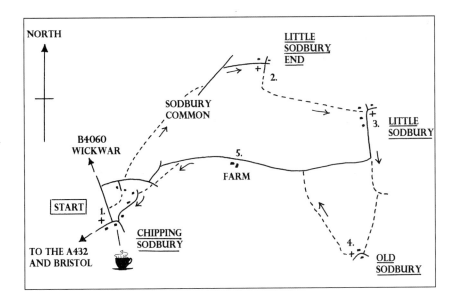

with 'Frome Valley Walkway' signs. In 100 yards, at a junction with a tarmac path, turn left to pass through the estate. Where this path joins Couzens Close, keep straight ahead to the junction with the Chipping Sodbury Bypass. Turn right and, in 150 yards, with Dowding Close on the right, cross the main road to reach a stile in the hedgerow opposite. Cross the field beyond this stile to a gateway in the opposite hedgerow, before crossing the next field to a stile in the far right corner and the driveway leading to the local golf course. Turn left and, in just 20 yards, fork right onto Chipping Sodbury Common. Follow the line of a hedgerow across the Common and, where this hedge ends, keep ahead across the Common for ½ mile to join the road by Newhouse Farm. Turn left and, in 250 yards, turn right along a side turning to follow the lane into Little Sodbury End. Continue for ¼ mile to a cattle grid and a road junction in this small hamlet.

2. At this junction, just past a chapel, turn right along a cul de sac lane to reach a gate/stile alongside a bungalow. Continue along the left edge of a field for 100 yards to a handgate on the left. Pass through this gate and, in the next field, head across to a stile in the middle of the opposite field boundary, 100 yards to the right of Winchcombe Farm. In the next field, head across to a stile in the opposite field boundary, almost in the bottom right corner. In the following field, cross to a stile in the far left corner, before heading straight across the following field to a stile in the opposite hedgerow, walking in line with the clearly visible Little Sodbury church. Follow the left edge of the next field to a stile in the top left corner. In one final field, head across to a stile immediately past a property on the left, before passing through some scrubland to reach a stile and the lane in Little Sodbury by the church.

Little Sodbury Manor, lying in a sheltered location beneath the Cotswold escarpment, has played host to the rich, the powerful and the famous over the years. In 1535, the then owner Sir John Walsh entertained Henry VIII and Anne Boleyn whilst en route to Bristol. A few years earlier, William Tyndale, who was later to translate the New Testament, was chaplain and tutor to Sir John's children. Naturally, the local feeling is that much of the preparatory work for this translation was done whilst Tyndale resided at Little Sodbury. The village church, standing on the former village green, is the only one in this country dedicated to St Adeline. Other than the church and manor, Little Sodbury consists of no more than a few scattered stone-built farmhouses and cottages.

3. Turn right along the lane, and head uphill out of Little Sodbury. In 600 yards, where the lane bears right by a waterboard installation, fork left along a footpath to Old Sodbury. In 300 yards, where this path bears left to climb the escarpment, bear right off the path to a stile. You are

Broad Street, Chipping Sodbury

now on a section of the Cotswold Way. Head across the bottom of a hillside field for 600 yards to a stile in the far right corner, before continuing along an enclosed path to Cotswold Lane in Old Sodbury by the church. Turn right, pass through the churchyard, and continue to a kissing gate in the wall just beyond the church.

Old Sodbury, nestling into the Cotswold escarpment, still manages to retain a certain rural charm despite its proximity to both Bath and Bristol. Inside the 800 year old St John the Baptist church are two fine effigies, both of knights, one dating from the 14th century unusually carved in wood, the other dating from the 13th century, carved in stone, the knight nearly swamped by his shield. Who these knights represent is unknown, but it is thought they could have been Lords of the Manor. The view from the churchyard is especially fine, with the Severn Vale and the distant Welsh Hills to the west, and the slopes of the Cotswold Hills stretching away to the north.

4. Follow the fieldpath downhill to the bottom left corner of the field, before turning right to follow the bottom field boundary for 100 yards to a stile just before a pond. Cross this stile and, in the next field, head across to a gate in the far right corner. Beyond this gate, cross another gate immediately on your right. Beyond this gate, bear half left, clipping the corner of a field, to a gate in the left-hand hedgerow. In the next field, turn right and walk the whole length of the field to a stile in the end field boundary. Head across the next two fields, crossing a gate in a fence along the way, to a gate that lies almost in the left corner of the second field. Join a lane, turn left and continue for ¼ mile to a cattle grid by Harwoodgate Farm and Sodbury Common.

☕ **5.** Follow the road across the Common for 600 yards and, just past a property on the left, cross a stile on the left. You are now on a section of the Monarch's Way. Follow the right edge of the field ahead towards the housing estates of Chipping Sodbury. In the far right corner of this field, cross a stile and a footbridge and, in the next field, walk directly ahead to a stile and a bridge over a stream before joining the main road that serves as the Chipping Sodbury Bypass. Turn right, pass the entrance to Manor Way and, just before the River Frome, turn left to follow the path that runs along the backs of houses by the river for 200 yards to join Hatters Lane. Turn left, and follow the pavement through a light industrial estate for 300 yards until the lane bears left to join Broad Street in the centre of Chipping Sodbury. Turn right — you will soon pass Poppy's Tea Rooms on the left — before taking the first right into Wickwar Road to return to the car park.

Walk 4
DYRHAM and WEST LITTLETON

The Cotswold escarpment marks the divide between the high undulating Cotswold plateau and the low-lying flood plain of the Severn Vale. In centuries past, the hilltops were home to the Cotswold sheep farmers, with the occasional fold in the landscape being the site of the odd hamlet or farmstead. The larger villages tended to lie in the shelter of the escarpment, looking out across the Severn Vale. This walk in and around what is known colloquially as the 'Cotswold Edge' examines this delightful corner of South Gloucestershire. As well as the fine views westwards to the River Severn and beyond, there are the traditional Cotswold stone villages of Dyrham and West Littleton. Be sure to pick a fine, clear day for what can be a breezy stroll across the Cotswold hilltops.

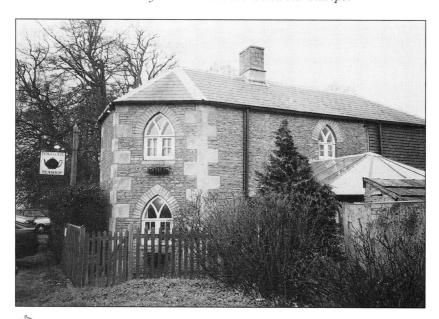

The former coach road from Bath to Gloucester — known today rather less romantically as the A46 — used to run across the Cotswold hilltops high above the Severn Vale. Dotted along the way was the occasional tollhouse, where travellers would pay their dues for the use and upkeep of the highway. The one-time tollhouse above Dyrham is now home to the Tollgate Teashop, whose traditional stone and beamed interior provides welcoming rest and refreshment for motorists travelling to and from the nearby M4 motorway. Morning coffee, afternoon teas and light lunches are provided, the latter typically including homemade soup and filled jacket potatoes. In addition to scones and teacakes, such tempting options as apple cake, mince slice, carrot cake, banana cake and chocolate cake are available. A conservatory extension, as well as a garden area, makes the Tollgate Teashop quite the perfect stopping-off point halfway around this walk in the Southern Cotswolds. Open during normal business hours, seven days a week. Telephone: 01225 891585.

DISTANCE: 5½ miles.
MAPS: OS Landranger 172 or Explorer 155.
STARTING POINT: The rest and picnic area on the A46 immediately to the south of junction 18 of the M4 motorway (GR 757778).
HOW TO GET THERE: Follow the A46 north from Bath towards the M4 motorway. Immediately before reaching junction 18 of the M4, a left turn gives access to a large parking and picnic area. If coming from Bristol, leave the M4 at junction 18, and follow the A46 towards Bath. Almost immediately, a right turn gives access to the picnic area.

The Walk

1. Leave the car park, walk back to the A46 and cross the main road with care to reach a footpath opposite. Follow what is an enclosed green lane for 300 yards until the track reaches an open field. Follow the right edges of the next two fields to a country lane. Cross the old stile opposite, before crossing to the far left corner of the next field where the footpath joins an unmetalled track. Follow this track to the south for ½ mile to its junction with the West Littleton road. Turn left along this lane, and continue for 600 yards to a telephone box in West Littleton. Turn right, and follow a footpath up to the church, before continuing through the churchyard to a stile in the end boundary wall. Continue along an enclosed path — a horse paddock on the right — to a handgate, before crossing a field to a gateway opposite. Ahead, steps and a horse jump cross a wall. Do not cross this wall — instead, pass through a handgate on the left into the adjoining field.

Arthur Mee, in his guidebook to Gloucestershire published in 1938, described West Littleton as 'a small place very high, with delightful old farm buildings and a splendid barn with weathered tiles'. There is also the enchanting church tucked

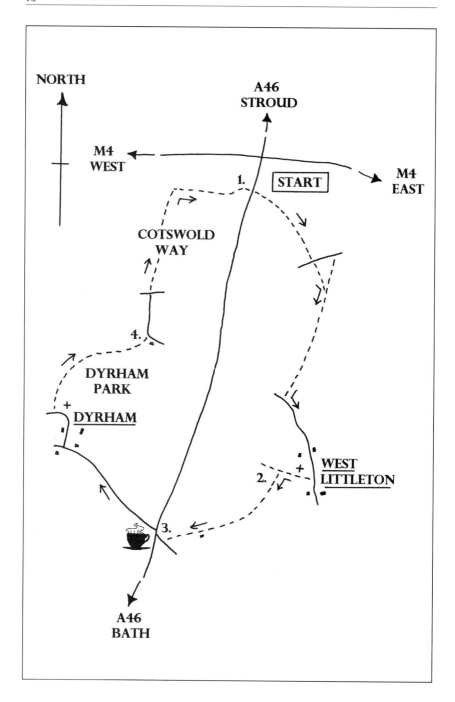

away off the main road through the village, which has a lovely canopied niche above the doorway, with very worn figures of Mary and Jesus, as well as a massive bellcot that is believed to be over 700 years old.

☕ **2.** Follow the left-hand field boundary across the top of this field to a gap in the hedge just a few yards down from the far left corner. In the next field, continue following the left-hand field boundary to a wooden fence in the far left corner. Cross this wooden barrier, and immediately turn right through a gateway on the right. Follow the left edges of the next two fields to reach a stone barn. Pass to the right of this barn, and continue ahead following the field boundary on the left to reach a gate in the corner of the field. Beyond this gate, follow the edge of a copse down to a stile and a lane. Turn right, and walk the short distance to the A46. The Tollgate Teashop is 150 yards to the left along the A46, which you should cross with both patience and care!

3. From the teashop, turn left and take the next lane on the left — opposite the one by which you reached the A46 — and follow it downhill into Dyrham. Turn right at the first junction in Dyrham, and follow a back lane around past Dyrham House and the entrance to the church. Continue along the lane for another 50 yards to a right turn signposted 'Cotswold Way'. Turn right, and follow a section of track up to a gate and open fields. Follow the right edges of the next five fields, bordering Dyrham Park, to reach a lane alongside a National Trust compound.

Dyrham is best known for its rather grand manor house, now a National Trust property. The mansion was built for William Blathwayt, Secretary at War and Secretary of State to William III, between 1691 and 1702. The rooms have changed very little since they were furnished by Blathwayt, when their contents were recorded in his housekeeper's inventory. Around the house lies 263 acres of ancient parkland, home to a herd of fallow deer. The house is open from April to October (telephone: 01179 372501).

4. Turn left, and follow this lane for 300 yards to the next junction. Enter the field opposite — signposted as the Cotswold Way — and follow the left edges of two fields across the hilltop. At the far side of the second field, pass through a gateway and turn right to follow the right edge of the next field up towards an aerial mast and some woodland. On reaching the trees, continue following the edge of the field alongside the woodland up to the corner of the field. Bear left,

Dyrham House is a National Trust property

and follow the end field boundary around to a gravel path on the right. Follow this path back into the picnic area and car park.

The Cotswold Way follows the Cotswold escarpment from Chipping Campden in a southerly direction to the City of Bath. The views along the way are quite spectacular, extending across the Severn Vale towards the distant Welsh Hills. The section of the Cotswold Way followed from Dyrham back to the picnic area is no exception to this rule. From the breezy hilltops, the views are never less than impressive.

Walk 5
CASTLE COMBE

Back in 1962, Castle Combe received the accolade of being 'the prettiest village in England'. Since then, the awards have come in thick and fast, the latest being from the North American magazine 'British Heritage' whose readers, in a recent vote, decided that the village was the most picturesque place in Britain. There can be no denying the photogenic qualities of this most beautiful of villages, with its ranks of stone cottages lining the main street as it climbs from the ancient bridge over the By Brook up to the ancient market cross. Away from the village, this walk explores a wooded landscape watered by both the By Brook and its tributaries. There are plunging valleys, steep wooded slopes and a degree of solitude that contrasts markedly with the crowds back in Castle Combe itself.

Having emerged from the By Brook valley onto the course of the Foss Way, the walk passes Foss Farm. The traditional Cotswold farmhouse, with its pleasant gardens, is now home to a most delightful tearoom. On warm, sunny days, the front garden is an idyllic spot to rest and linger awhile over a fine cup of tea, whilst the front room of the farmhouse, with its tables adorned in pretty checked tablecloths, offers warmth and shelter should the weather be less inviting. As well as a good selection of teas — that typically include Indian, Assam and Earl Grey — Foss Farm also offers coffees, cream teas, toasted teacakes and a variety of pastries. If your appetite demands something more substantial, there is also a selection of sandwiches as well as traditional pasties. Foss Farm also offers residential accommodation, where visitors can enjoy the delights of the excellent meals available to guests. Open from 10.30 am every day. Telephone: 01249 782286.

DISTANCE: 4½ miles.
MAPS: OS Landranger 173 or Explorer 156.
STARTING POINT: The public car park in Upper Castle Combe (GR 845777).
HOW TO GET THERE: Upper Castle Combe lies on the B4039 road between Old Sodbury and Chippenham. The car park is clearly signposted from the main road.

THE WALK

1. Leave the car park, turn right and then right again at the next junction to follow the lane leading down into Castle Combe. In just 50 yards, fork right off this road just past a property on the left called Hillside Cottage. Walk along a side lane, past cottages and the old school until, where the lane bears right, cross an old stile on the left-hand side. Follow the left edge of an enclosure until the path emerges onto the local golf course. Continue along this path which shortly drops downhill to reach a stile in the wall ahead. Do not cross the stile — instead turn right and follow a wooded path alongside a stone wall until the path re-emerges onto the golf course greens. Follow the grassy path ahead to its junction with a tarmac path, before turning right and continuing to a bridge over the By Brook. Cross the river, and continue along the tarmac path until, in 150 yards, just past the tee mat for hole 4, fork left along a signposted footpath. Follow this path alongside Broadmead Brook until it emerges at a set of gates and Nettleton Mill.

The By Brook is one of the most attractive of the Bristol Avon's tributaries. From its source near Tormarton in South Gloucestershire, it flows down through Castle Combe, Ford, Slaughterford and Box — a veritable Who's Who of Cotswold settlements — to its confluence with the River Avon at Bathford on the edge of Bath. The clear waters of the By Brook offer fine sport to local fishermen, whilst the wooded habitats along its course make it a magnet for ornithologists.

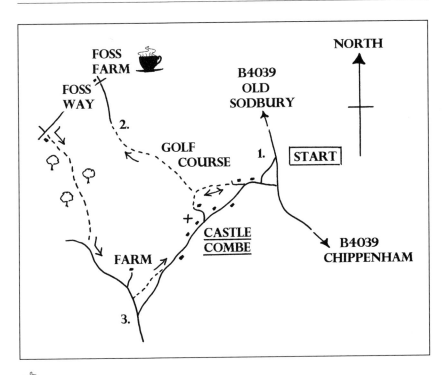

2. Follow the lane ahead between properties uphill for 600 yards to reach a road junction by Foss Farm and the tearoom. To continue, turn left and walk along the lane for 600 yards to the next junction, before turning left along a track that runs alongside Foss Cottage. Follow this track for 300 yards down to a clapper bridge over Broadmead Brook. Cross this bridge, and follow the track up out of the valley and on for ½ mile to a lane. Turn left, and follow this lane for ½ mile until, 150 yards past the impressive driveway leading to Shrub Farm, turn left over a stile — there is no signpost — into Becker's Wood.

The Foss Way, the ancient Roman road, runs from Lincolnshire to the Devon coast. Although largely incorporated into the modern road network, one or two sections of green lane remain along the way which still exude a sense of history, where one can almost visualise the Roman legions stepping out across Britain. Unfortunately, the section of the Foss Way followed on this walk has long been covered in tarmac.

3. Follow the path through the woodland for 500 yards until it drops down and joins the Ford to Castle Combe lane. Turn left into Castle

Combe, and walk up the main street as far as the market cross. Fork left up past the Castle Inn and pass under the arch alongside Arch Cottage. Continue along a back lane that bears left and then right before turning into a property. At this point, keep ahead uphill along a footpath that passes under a bridge before reaching a stile passed earlier in the walk. Cross this stile, and retrace your steps along the path ahead which climbs up to the golf course, before passing the former village school en route back to the car park.

First time visitors to Castle Combe inevitably experience a sense of déjà vu, pictures of the village having appeared on any number of chocolate boxes, greetings cards and calendars. Film buffs will also recognise the village, which featured in the 1966 version of 'Doctor Doolittle'. The By Brook and its adjoining cottages were transformed into the diminutive fishing village that was the focal point for this 20th Century Fox movie. It is the medieval domestic architecture that most catches the eye, however. The ranks of cottages, all crafted from mellow Cotswold limestone, each with its gables and dormer windows, were the home of weavers and spinners in centuries past. As in much of the West Country, it was the wool trade on which Castle Combe's prosperity was originally founded. The market cross was the focal point of village life, being the spot where traders would gather each Monday touting their wares to all and sundry.

Castle Combe, 'the prettiest village in England'

Walk 6
MARSHFIELD and WEST LITTLETON

*H*igh *on the Cotswold plateau above Bath and Bristol sits the village of Marshfield, whose long main street is lined with ancient cottages, houses and inns. From the heart of the village, the walk sets out to explore this undulating landscape, with its traditional farms and their dry-stone walls stretching away across the countryside. Such is the nature of the landscape that many a writer has likened it to the Derbyshire Dales or the North Yorkshire Moors. Along the way lies just one settlement — at West Littleton — little more than a few houses and a church that lie in a sheltered dip. This pleasant rural excursion is indeed far from the madding crowd.*

Sweetapples, a delightful teashop in the heart of Marshfield's High Street, occupies what is thought to be the site of a former malthouse. Internally, there is exposed stonework and traditional beams, as well as an open fireplace that houses a wood burning stove. Around the walls of the tearoom are a number of old black and white photographs of Marshfield, as well as display cupboards of traditional pots, china and other old-fashioned artifacts. Sweetapples offers teas and coffees, as well as full English breakfasts, baguettes, sandwiches, baked potatoes and a good selection of homemade cakes. These might include chocolate cake and butterfly cakes or caramel shortbread and sticky chocolate cake. Lovers of the traditional English cream tea will not be disappointed, either! It is altogether a perfect refreshment stop in a handsome Cotswold stone village. Open during normal business hours, excluding Sundays. Telephone: 01225 891657. Alternative refreshments in Marshfield can be found at the Crown Inn, located in the main street almost opposite the tearoom. As well as beers, soft drinks and coffees, the Crown serves sandwiches, soup and a wide range of cooked food.

DISTANCE: 6 miles.

MAPS: OS Landranger 172 or Explorer 155.

STARTING POINT: Sweetapples Teashop at the eastern end of Marshfield's High Street. There is roadside parking all of the way along the High Street (GR 779737).

HOW TO GET THERE: The A420 road from Bristol to Chippenham effectively bypasses Marshfield. As you approach Marshfield, leave the main road and follow the signs to the centre of the village. Drive to the eastern end of the High Street where you will find Sweetapples almost opposite the Crown Inn.

THE WALK

In the tax assessment of 1334, Marshfield was surprisingly the fourth highest source of revenue in the county after Bristol, Gloucester and Cirencester. The former importance of the village, a one-time coaching post on the London to Bristol route, can be seen by a cursory glance at the impressive High Street. This stretches for some ½ mile from the early 17th century almshouses at the western end to 'the market' by the village church at the eastern end of the village. The large Perpendicular church dates from the 15th century and houses a rather handsome Jacobean pulpit. Visit Marshfield on Boxing Day and the High Street is alive to the sights and sounds of a Mummers' Play.

1. Walk the length of Marshfield's High Street until, just before the almshouses, turn right into George Lane and walk up to the A420. Cross

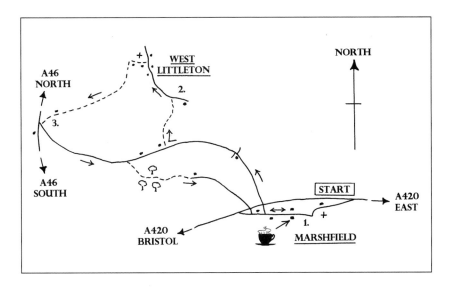

the main road, and follow the lane opposite signposted to Castle Farm. At the crossroads by Castle Farm, keep directly ahead along the lane signposted to Dyrham and Doynton to reach Springs Farm in 600 yards. Just before the farmhouse, turn right to follow a signposted footpath. Follow this footpath alongside the farmhouse and on up the left edge of a field to a stone slab stile in the top left corner. Beyond this stile, follow the right edge of the next field to some steps over the wall in the right-hand corner, before dropping downhill to a gate at the bottom of the slope. Continue uphill to a gate at the top of the field, before continuing along a grassy track — Cadwellhill Barn away to the right — to reach another gate and a lane.

2. Turn left into West Littleton and, upon reaching a telephone box, turn left to the village church. Pass to the left of the church to a stile, before continuing ahead alongside a riding paddock to a handgate and a small field. Cross this field to a gateway opposite. In the enclosure beyond this gate, pass through a handgate ahead just to the left of some steps over a wall. Follow the top left edge of the next field for 350 yards to a gap in the hedge in the far left corner. In the next field, follow the left-hand field boundary for 200 yards to the far left corner, then cross a wooden barrier on the left before crossing a gate on the right and following the left edge of the adjoining field. At the far side of this field, pass through another gateway and continue ahead to Littleton Wood Barn. Pass to the right of the barn and continue following the left edge of the field to a gate in the corner by Littleton Wood. Follow the edge of this wood for a short distance to a gate and a lane, a little way from the busy A46.

West Littleton is a diminutive settlement lying in a sheltered dip in the high wolds. Contemporary guidebooks rarely seem to refer to the village, although it does rate a reference in Arthur Mee's 'Gloucestershire' in the King's England series. West Littleton is referred to here as 'a small place very high, with delightful old farm buildings'. Arthur Mee also noted that 'the most precious heritage is in the church, a lovely canopied niche above the doorway, with very worn figures of Mary and Jesus ... probably 600 years old.'

☕ **3.** Turn left, and follow this lane for ¾ mile. Just before Middledown House, fork right onto a bridleway and drop downhill to a gate. Continue following the bridleway ahead as it climbs up through the trees. On emerging into a hillside field, drop downhill to a footbridge over Broadmead Brook. Pass through the gateway ahead and continue along a track uphill to the lane by Westend Town Farm. Follow this lane for

The 17th century almshouses at Marshfield

150 yards to Westend Farm, before continuing along the lane ahead to reach the A420. Cross the main road, and follow the lane opposite down to the western end of Marshfield's High Street by a former tollhouse. Turn left, and retrace your steps along the High Street back to Sweetapples.

Many diminutive watercourses have their origins on the high wolds. The appropriately named Springs Farm sits above a small valley whose springs give rise to Broadmead Brook, one of the Bristol Avon's lesser known tributaries. Towards journey's end, one of those springs is passed and it is everything a spring should be. There is an exposed rockface from whose base a crystal clear and pure source of water comes bubbling forth.

Walk 7
CORSHAM and WESTROP

One of the undoubted delights of the English countryside is the grand country house or manor set in its rolling acres of manicured parkland. At Corsham, a market town deep in the Wiltshire countryside, we find Corsham Court, with its gables and mullioned windows, its pediments and pinnacles. From the Court — and its adjoining church — the walk heads across Corsham Park to the neighbouring hamlet of Westrop. Little more than a scattering of cottages and farms, the golden stone used as the building blocks in each dwelling gives the place a real Cotswold feel and charm. Beyond Westrop, the route re-enters Corsham Park where the footpath borders a fine stretch of open water. Many breeds of wildfowl make their home on Corsham Lake, including a splendid flock of Canada geese. This is altogether a pleasant rural stroll that will leave you feeling part of the landed gentry... if only for a day!

Corsham's High Street is lined with an attractive array of 17th and 18th-century buildings, fashioned from the cream coloured Bath stone which has now mellowed to perfection. Number 8 in the High Street is a bistro which, in daytime hours, also serves an excellent range of teas and coffees. Internally, the exposed stonework and beams lend 'No 8' a most traditional feel. The variety of teas offered includes Assam, English Breakfast Tea, Ceylon, Darjeeling and Earl Grey. There is also the option of everlasting refills! In addition, customers can enjoy a selection of coffees, as well as hot chocolate and soft drinks. To accompany your beverages, the menu includes scones, teacakes, pastries, a selection of cakes, toast and much more besides. Should your appetite demand something more substantial, a good range of lunches is available at 'No 8', as well as the option of a good old English cooked breakfast. Open during normal business hours, seven days a week. Telephone: 01249 701190.

DISTANCE: 3½ miles.

MAPS: OS Landranger 173 or Explorer 156.

STARTING POINT: The parking area alongside Corsham Court and Corsham church (GR 873706).

HOW TO GET THERE: The A4 between Bath and Chippenham borders the northern fringes of the Wiltshire market town of Corsham. From the A4 along the edge of the town, follow the brown tourist signs for Corsham Court. These direct you to the northern end of the High Street, where a left turn into Church Street will bring you to Corsham Court.

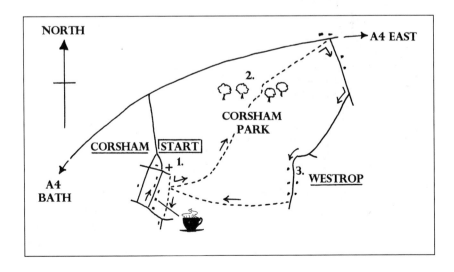

THE WALK

1. Leave the parking area via the kissing gate that gives access to the tree-lined South Avenue. Almost immediately, cross a stile on the left-hand side and enter Corsham Park. Bear half left, and follow the footpath that runs alongside the churchyard wall. On reaching the end corner of this wall, continue across Corsham Park, bearing slightly to the left. The path soon runs alongside a ha-ha and a hedgerow on the left. Follow this field boundary to a gate in the corner of the field. Beyond this gate, continue along an enclosed footpath for 250 yards to the next gate and enter the corner of the adjoining field. Follow the left edge of this field for 250 yards to a marker post on the left. Beyond this post bear half right, clipping the corner of the field, to reach a stile in the end field boundary 200 yards from the left-hand corner of the field. Cross the paddock ahead to a clearly visible post just before a belt of woodland. Follow the track through this woodland to a gate and a stile that gives access to the next section of Corsham Park.

Thomas Smythe originally built Corsham Court, home of the Methuen family, in 1582 on the site of an earlier manor house. The Methuen family, prosperous woollen traders, purchased the property in 1745. In 1760, 'Capability' Brown built the state rooms and laid out the extensive parkland, whilst Humphry Repton made extensive alterations to the grounds some 40 years later. As well as marvelling at the Elizabethan appearance of the south face of Corsham Court, visitors are equally impressed with the splendid displays in the state rooms. These are 17th-century Flemish paintings as well as a famous collection of English furniture, including handsome pieces by Chippendale and Robert Adam.

2. Head across the parkland to the far left-hand corner some ½ mile distant, passing through a gate in a boundary fence partway across the parkland. In the far left corner of Corsham Park, pass through a gateway in the boundary wall to reach a road junction where the lane from Easton joins the busy A4. Turn right along Easton Road, and continue for 600 yards to the next junction. Turn right along a side turning, and continue for ½ mile into Westrop, ignoring one left turn along the way.

3. Pass through Westrop and, just 100 yards beyond this hamlet, cross a stile on the right into a paddock. Cross this paddock to the gateway opposite, and follow the enclosed path beyond to a stile and another entrance to Corsham Park. Cross the parkland ahead — initially detouring to the right to follow the permissive path that runs alongside Corsham Lake. In the far right corner of the parkland, some ½ mile

Corsham Court glimpsed from Corsham Lake

distant, cross a stile just to the left of the church to rejoin the South Avenue. Turn left, and follow South Avenue down to a gate at its southern end. Turn right along the B3353 Pickwick Road, and continue as far as the Methuen Arms. Just beyond this hotel, turn right into the High Street. Almost immediately, the bistro, 'No 8', is on the right-hand side. Head to the far end of the High Street, before turning right into Church Street to return to the parking area.

Corsham owes much of its origins and wealth to the West of England woollen trade. The large number of handsome 17th and 18th-century properties that line the High Street are fashioned from the golden limestone that for centuries was mined in the area. Indeed, one working stone mine still operates on the edge of the town, whilst a former mine is now open to the public as a tourist attraction. Fine weavers' cottages, dating from the 15th century, gabled and with mullioned windows, line the northern end of the High Street, whilst on Pickwick Road lie a block of L-shaped almshouses. Founded in 1668 by Margaret Hungerford, the almshouses also include the master's house. Visitors keen to discover more about Corsham and its history — the woollen trade, the stone mines and the many historical buildings — will find a Visitors' Centre in the High Street.

Walk 8
LACOCK and REYBRIDGE

*L*acock, a few miles east of Bath in the Wiltshire countryside, is a National Trust village of international repute. The medieval street plan, the local abbey, St Cyriac's church and a host of magnificent buildings attract tens of thousands of visitors each year. Whilst the village itself could easily fill several hours of your time, this walk also provides the opportunity to explore a stretch of the River Avon as it meanders its way across the local floodplain from neighbouring Reybridge.

 In the heart of Lacock, just a few yards from the church, stands King John's Hunting Lodge, a centuries old cottage which now houses a most delightful tearoom. Small beamed rooms, with polished tables and wooden chairs, provide a welcoming atmosphere for the thirsty visitor. As well as traditional cream teas, tea and cake, tea and toast, plain tea and child's tea, there is an extraordinary option known as 'Royal Tea'. This consists of smoked salmon and cucumber sandwiches, homemade scones, clotted cream, full fruit jam, dropped scones from the griddle and dainty cakes. Even after an exhilarating walk in the local countryside, this would provide some challenge even to the most ravenous of appetites! Light lunches are served, including homemade soup and a range of sandwiches. There is also a King John's Trencher — savoury potato cakes with a cheesy topping, served with freshly prepared salad. Open during normal business hours, every day in the summer months, weekends only in winter. Telephone: 01249 730313.

DISTANCE: 2½ miles.

MAPS: OS Landranger 173 or Explorer 156.

STARTING POINT: The signposted public car park on the edge of Lacock (GR 917683)

HOW TO GET THERE: Lacock lies just to the east of the A350 trunk road, midway between Chippenham and Melksham. The village is clearly signposted from the main road, as is the public car park.

THE WALK

1. Leave the car park and follow the road to the right out of Lacock. In 300 yards, having crossed a causeway and the first of two stone bridges across the River Avon and its floodplain, cross a stone slab stile on the left into an open field. Cross this field to a stile/footbridge in the end field boundary, alongside a telegraph pole. In the next field, follow the hedgerow on the left as far as a gate. Beyond this gate, follow a line of telegraph poles across the next field to reach a gate/stile. Drop down to the banks of the River Avon beyond this stile, and follow the river upstream across two further fields to reach a stile and the lane in Reybridge alongside the river.

The Bristol Avon between Lacock and Reybridge meanders across a flat clay vale that, in the days before flood relief schemes and sluice gates, would have been frequently underwater. This is evident from the raised causeways at both Reybridge and Lacock. An assortment of flora and fauna have made their home along this section of the river — it should not be difficult in the summer months to spot dragonflies, water lilies, teasels and moorhen along the course of the river, with timid rabbits feeding alongside in the riverside meadows.

2. Cross the River Avon, and turn left in front of a cottage. Shortly, where the road bears right, keep ahead between two cottages along a tarmac path to reach a kissing gate and an open field above the River Avon. Follow the tarmac footpath across this field to reach a wooden gate by some cottages on the far side of the field.

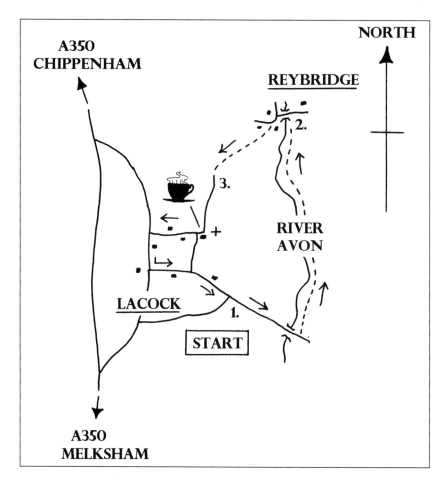

The tarmac path back across the fields from Reybridge to Lacock runs slightly above the level of the river, giving extensive views to the east. Immediately at hand is the Avon, beyond which — and several hundred feet higher — lie Naish and Bowden Hills, rising to a height of nearly 600 feet above sea-level (the Avon here is just 150 feet above sea-level). The more gentle slopes of this higher land are given over to arable farming, with woodland emerging on the higher slopes.

☕ **3.** Turn left beyond this gate, and follow a back lane down into Lacock, crossing a tributary stream of the River Avon before reaching St Cyriac's church. Turn right, and walk the whole length of Church Street to its junction with West Street, passing King John's Hunting Lodge along the way. Turn left along West Street, before taking the first left into

Lacock's High Street. Walk the whole length of the High Street as far as the Red Lion Inn, before continuing along the road past the entrance to the abbey, back to the car park.

The village of Lacock dates back to Saxon times, if not earlier, and has been described as 'easily the most remarkable and the most beautiful village in Wiltshire'. The village is based around four streets — Church Street, West and East Streets and the High Street — and still very much resembles a medieval town. Lacock's attractive houses cover every century from the 13th to the 18th, with little more recent development to spoil the overall effect. There is so much to see in the village — the abbey, the tithe barn, the Fox Talbot Museum of Photography, St Cyriac's church, the village cross, the packhorse bridge, and so on — that the walk and a refreshment break at King John's Hunting Lodge will inevitably only form a part of your day out.

Lacock Abbey was founded in the 13th century

Walk 9
ROWDE and THE KENNET
AND AVON CANAL

When the Kennet and Avon Canal reached the western approaches to Devizes, there was just one minor problem — the question of how to ascend Caen Hill. The initial solution, a tramline, was soon dropped in favour of a flight of locks. It all sounds so simple until one realises that this is no ordinary flight — rather it is a staircase of 16 consecutive locks, the most spectacular series of locks in the country. Before the opportunity to explore this unique piece of canal architecture, the walk heads across country to the little village of Rowde. The whole scene lies in the shadow of Roundway Hill, site of a Civil War battle in 1643. Local lore maintains that the victorious Royalists originally named the site 'Runaway Hill' on account of the fleeing Parliamentary forces!

☕ Towards the top of the Caen Hill flight of locks — actually alongside lock number 44 — a diminutive red-brick property lies almost hidden in the trees on the canal bank. Originally a lock keeper's cottage, this property is now home to the Lock Cottage Tea Rooms. Internally, there are two rooms — the serving area with its associated gift shop and an adjoining room where customers can sit and enjoy their food and drink. On fine days, however, most visitors head for the picnic tables in the garden, where a traditional English cuppa can be enjoyed whilst overlooking the passing boat traffic negotiating the Caen Hill locks. As well as tea, coffee and soft drinks, the Lock Cottage Tea Rooms offers patrons a varied selection of nibbles. These might typically include toasted teacakes, scones, slices of homemade cake, ice creams and a range of chocolate bars. It is worth spending a few minutes perusing the wares in the gift shop, which range from postcards and prints through to guidebooks and decorative china. An idyllic tearoom in an idyllic location alongside one of the wonders of the waterways world. Open during normal business hours, seven days a week. Telephone: 01380 724880.

DISTANCE: 4 miles.

MAPS: OS Landranger 173 or Explorer 156.

STARTING POINT: Caen Hill Locks car park (GR 984616).

HOW TO GET THERE: Initially aim for Rowde, on the A342 Chippenham to Devizes road. In the centre of the village, turn southwards by the Cross Keys Inn onto the B3101. In just ½ mile, a signposted left turn leads to the Caen Hill car park.

THE WALK

1. Retrace your steps down the unmetalled track to the B3101. Turn right, and follow the footpath alongside the B3101 for ½ mile to its junction with the A342 by the Cross Keys in Rowde. Turn left, and follow the A342 for 100 yards to the George and Dragon pub. Immediately before this hostelry, turn left and follow the footpath up to the church and Old Vicarage. Continue to a gate at the southern end of the churchyard, and continue ahead to reach Rowde Court Road. Turn right, and follow this road through a modern housing estate for 200 yards.

The prominent hill a mile or so to the north, visible during the early part of the walk, is Roundway Hill. The magnificent escarpment marks the divide between the chalk uplands of the North Wessex Downs and the clay vale of the Bristol Avon. Down in the vale stands the small village of Rowde, where St Matthew's

45

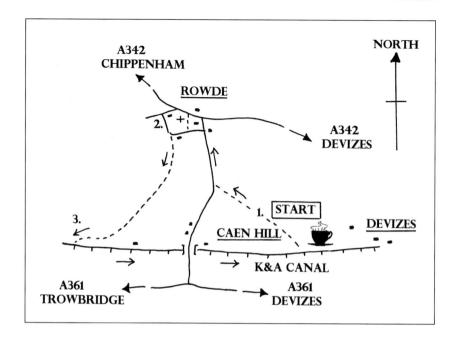

church dates back to the 12th century, although the fine tower was added some 300 years later. Perhaps Rowde's most famous residents were the Bartholomew family. John Smith Bartholomew and his brother-in-law Henry Wadworth set up Wadworth's, the well-known Devizes brewery.

2. Where Rowde Court Road bears right at the end of the estate, turn left along a bridleway. In 200 yards, keep on this track as it bears right before continuing for another ½ mile to a point where the track reaches a stile. Cross this stile, turn right and follow the right edge of a field down to a stile in the bottom corner just past a pond. Cross the stile, walk up to the canal bank, turn right and continue as far as a lock. Cross the footbridge at the bottom end of this lock to join the towpath.

3. Turn left, and follow the towpath for ½ mile to the B3101 overbridge. Pass under the bridge, and follow the towpath ahead uphill as far as lock 41, Boto X Lock. For the teashop, continue beside the canal until you reach Lock 44 and Lock Cottage, a more than worthwhile diversion! To complete the walk, return to Lock 41, cross the canal and follow the grassy ride ahead between the side pounds to a gap in the hedge opposite. Pass through this gap to return to the car park.

Some of the 29 locks near Devizes on the Kennet and Avon Canal

To reach Devizes from the west, the Kennet and Avon Canal faced an ascent of some 237 feet from the Avon Vale into the town. Within a distance of little more than two miles, 29 locks were constructed, including the 16 in quick succession as the canal climbed up through Caen Hill. One question that is always asked by visitors is how long it would take a barge to negotiate the Caen Hill Staircase? J.T. Ferris, who in years gone by ran a narrowboat between Newbury and Bristol, allegedly set the record. He is reported to have worked his way up through these locks on one occasion in just 2½ hours!

Walk 10
BRADFORD-ON-AVON and AVONCLIFF

Without doubt, Bradford-on-Avon is one of the finest small towns in Britain. With its ancient churches, a vast tithe barn, former weavers' cottages and rather grand mill owners' houses, all lovingly crafted from the local golden limestone, it is not difficult to see why the town has been described as 'Bath in miniature'. This walk explores the countryside to the north and west of Bradford where, in addition to the picturesque hamlets of Turleigh and Avoncliff, we find a section of the Kennet and Avon Canal, an impressive aqueduct, secluded deciduous woodland and some glorious views across the West Wiltshire countryside. There is a short, steep climb out of Bradford at the outset, but this is a small price to pay for the many delights that lie ahead further along the way.

☕ The Café at the Lock Inn, alongside the Kennet and Avon Canal in Bradford, was formerly a lengthman's cottage. Since 1990, however, it has evolved into one of the more unique and individual cafés in the area — if not the country. On hot, sunny days, customers can enjoy their food and drink at one of the many canalside tables, whilst on cooler days, there is plenty of warmth and shelter in the Lock Inn's cosy interior. The most recent addition to the accommodation is a restored canal boat, where patrons can quite literally enjoy their refreshments on the canal itself. Altogether a perfect spot to rest and linger awhile. An extensive menu is available, including a variety of teas, a range of coffees, cold drinks, cream teas and ice creams. This is only the start, however! Throughout the day, a vast range of hot food is offered, with the most famous dish being the 'Boatman's Breakfast'. This consists of bacon, egg, sausage, black pudding, smoked sausage, tomatoes, mushrooms, fried potatoes and fried bread. Such is the fame of this excellent meal that it has featured on television programmes in the region! After dark, the Lock Inn becomes a full-blown restaurant with a menu to match. Open during normal business hours, seven days a week; evening menu available from 6.30 pm. Telephone: 01225 868068.

DISTANCE: 4½ miles.

MAPS: OS Landranger 173 or Explorer 156. (A short section of the walk also creeps onto Landranger 172 or Explorer 155).

STARTING POINT: The station car park in Bradford-on-Avon (GR 824606).

HOW TO GET THERE: Bradford-on-Avon lies on the A363 between Bath and Trowbridge. Coming from Bath, cross the Town Bridge over the Avon and the second turning on the right is the entrance to the large station car park.

THE WALK

Bradford-on-Avon was historically a 'broad ford' through the River Avon. The town's wealth was founded upon the woollen trade, with any number of local mills being powered by the waters of the Avon. The town quite literally rises in steep tiers of dwellings above the river, an unforgettable sight when illuminated by the fading rays of an early autumn sunset. A fine stone bridge crosses the river, with two arches that date back as far as the 14th century. In the middle of the bridge is a small lock-up, which housed prisoners overnight whilst en route to gaols in Bristol and Salisbury. The Town Museum, housed above the local library, is a must for first time visitors to Bradford.

1. Return to the main A363, turn left and walk the short distance to Westbury Gardens, the public park alongside the River Avon and the Town Bridge in Bradford-on-Avon. Turn left, walk through Westbury

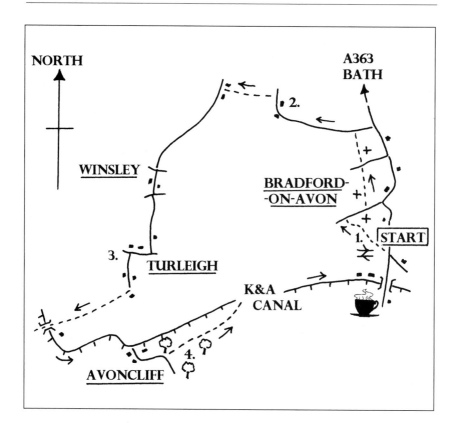

Gardens and pass through the archway in the bottom left corner that gives access to St Margaret's Hall car park. Continue alongside the river to a footbridge and cross the Avon. Turn left along Church Street — passing Holy Trinity church and the Saxon church — and, where Church Street ends, continue uphill along Church Lane to Barton Orchard. Continue ahead up Barton Steps to join Newtown. Turn right, and follow Newtown for 200 yards before turning left to climb Conigre Hill. At the top of the climb, having reached Winsley Road, follow Huntingdon Street opposite up to its junction with Ashley Road. Turn left, and follow Ashley Road for 400 yards to the Dog and Fox pub on the right.

Bradford's Saxon church is one of the best-preserved examples in the country, and was only discovered by chance! For many years, it lay hidden among a jumble of buildings, its original function lost in the mists of time. It was only in 1856, when a local vicar happened to look across the rooftops and espy a mysterious cross, that St Laurence once again became a place of worship. It is a plain building, as high as it is long, with very little by way of internal embellishment. In many ways, the beauty of the Saxon church lies in this very simplicity.

2. On the left, just past the Dog and Fox, is the driveway leading to Upper Bearfield Farm. Just past this driveway, cross a stile on the left and enter a large field. Head across to the far right corner of this field, before crossing a stone stile alongside a cottage to join Ashley Lane. Turn left, and follow Ashley Lane for ½ mile down to the Winsley Bypass. Cross the bypass to a handgate opposite, and continue down Ashley Lane to join Winsley Road. Turn right and in 15 yards, left down Cottles Lane. Follow Cottles Lane for 300 yards down to the next junction in Turleigh. Turn right and, in 150 yards, left into Green Lane.

Turleigh is one of the most desirable villages in the area. Consisting of a few old cottages and houses of mellow stone, tucked into the hillside above the Avon, this delightful hamlet has seen little recent development. Sadly, just about every single amenity in Turleigh has now closed down, leaving a number of properties with the appendage 'Old'. Look carefully, and you might find the 'Old Post Office' and the 'Old Malthouse' for example. It is very much a story of our times.

3. Continue along Green Lane, a cul de sac, until it ends by a property called Turleigh Croft. At this point, turn right and follow a track along to a gateway. Continue following this track across the top of a field to the next gate, before continuing along the track for ½ mile as it drops down the hillside into the Avon Valley to cross the Kennet and Avon Canal. Turn left, and follow the towpath for ½ mile into Avoncliff. Cross Avoncliff Aqueduct, pass the Madhatter Tearoom on the right and join a lane. Turn left, and follow this lane uphill out of Avoncliff.

Avoncliff is an isolated hamlet tucked away in one of the least accessible corners of the Avon Valley. Dominating the settlement is the 100 yard long aqueduct that carries the K&A Canal across the valley. Constructed of the local Bath stone, its essential features are three arches, a solid parapet and balustraded ends. The weir upstream of the aqueduct originally powered two local flock mills. Both still stand at either side of the weir, but in contrasting states of repair. The dereliction of the left-hand mill is in marked contrast to the handsome conversion that has turned its partner into a fine residence. Without doubt, the most popular attraction in Avoncliff is the Cross Guns Inn, an ancient hostelry that lies sandwiched between the River Avon and the Kennet and Avon Canal.

☕ **4.** In 250 yards, on a sharp right bend, bear left into woodland. Follow the signed path downhill through the trees. In 600 yards, cross a stile and enter a hillside field. Cross this field diagonally to a stile in the bottom left corner and, in the next field, follow the left-hand field boundary around to a stile and footbridge over a canal sluice. Continue along the footpath beyond the sluice for 250 yards to a footbridge, cross the canal and follow the towpath to the right for ½ mile to the Lock Inn Cottage and B3109. Turn left, and follow the main road for ¼ mile back into the centre of Bradford where the station car park is a left turn off the main road.

Bradford-on-Avon rises above the river Avon

Walk 11
WINSLEY and the AVON VALLEY

The Avon Valley between Bath and Bradford-on-Avon is widely held to offer some of the best walking country near to Bath. Steep wooded hillsides come tumbling down to the banks of the River Avon, whose constant companion in the valley bottom is the Kennet and Avon Canal. Scattered around the hillsides are the occasional hamlet or village, that add an element of human interest to this most attractive of landscapes. All of these elements — the canal, the hamlet of Murhill, the village of Winsley and the natural landscape in the form of the Murhill Bank Nature Reserve — combine to make this a most pleasing circular walk. There is one steep climb at the outset, but that is soon left behind and forgotten!

The final stretch of this delightful stroll follows the Kennet and Avon Canal deep in the heart of the Avon Valley. Just as the towpath approaches Winsley Hill Bridge and journey's end, a wooden gate in the hedgerow on the left marks the entrance to the Fordside Tea Gardens.

Tucked away in a corner of a garden — and surrounded by picnic tables and chairs — is a wooden chalet and the tearoom itself. Here thirsty visitors can enjoy tea, coffee and soft drinks, as well as a choice of delicious ice-creams. In addition to cream teas, the good selection of homemade cakes might well include lemon cake, chocolate cake, jam sponge and shortbread. With its spacious lawns and impressive views of the surrounding countryside, this is certainly a place to rest and linger awhile. Open during normal business hours, seven days a week, in the spring and summer months. Telephone: 01225 722115. Alternatively, if a warming meal is needed during the colder months, the Seven Stars pub in Winsley, which is passed on the route, also serves coffee, sandwiches, soup and rolls.

DISTANCE: 3½ miles.

MAPS: OS Landrangers 172 and 173 or Explorers 155 and 156.

STARTING POINT: The layby at the bottom of Winsley Hill, just below the Kennet and Avon Canal (GR 784613).

HOW TO GET THERE: Turn off the A36 Bath-Warminster road south of Bath at Monkton Combe, onto the B3108 Bradford-on-Avon road. In just over ½ mile, having passed under a railway bridge and over the River Avon, park on the left-hand side immediately before the Kennet and Avon Canal.

THE WALK

1. Walk up Winsley Hill on the pavement alongside the B3108 for 600 yards, before turning right along the lane signposted to Murhill. In 200 yards, just past a right turn to Murhill Farmhouse, bear left at a gravelled parking space into the Murhill Bank Nature Reserve. Continue along the 'perimeter path' beyond the information board, a path that runs parallel to the lane on the right. Follow this path — it soon enters woodland — for 600 yards until it rejoins Murhill Lane opposite a secluded parking space. Continue following the lane — ignoring all side turns — for 300 yards until, having climbed uphill, it joins Winsley Road in Winsley just past the entrance to Dorothy House Hospice.

Murhill Bank Nature Reserve consists of an acre of unimproved meadow, as well as a further acre of woodland. A small copse and a hedgerow border complete this collection of habitats. Unlike most British meadows, it has never been ploughed or sprayed, perhaps because it slopes so steeply, and it is these factors which have led to its richness of flora and fauna. An informative leaflet, available at the entrance to the reserve, details the wide variety of plants, butterflies, birds and animals to be found in and around the reserve. You may notice some exposed

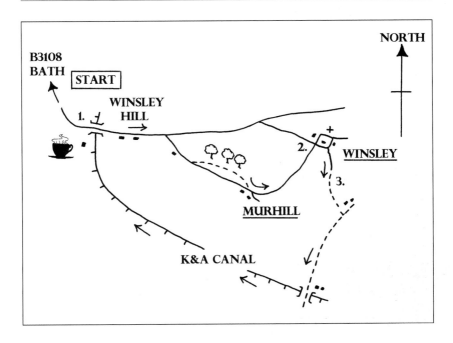

rock faces in Murhill. In the 18th and 19th centuries, stone from these quarries was brought down to a wharf at Murhill and trans-shipped into Bath. 'Murhill stone' was a name known in the trade — at least locally — although much of it was low quality stone.

2. Cross the road and follow the lane opposite past the entrance to Burghope Manor. Continue through the heart of 'old Winsley' before rejoining Winsley Road just past St Nicholas' church. Turn right, walk up past the Seven Stars Inn and, where the main road bears sharply right, keep ahead along a side lane signposted to the Village Hall and the Bowls Club. Continue along this lane as it bears first left and then right past the entrance to Chase View. Continue for 200 yards until the lane ends at a stone stile, with Winsley Cricket Club on the left and a footpath going off on the right.

Although dominated by modern housing, this walk passes through the heart of what is known locally as 'old Winsley'. A collection of delightful stone cottages and houses lie scattered around St Nicholas' church and the Seven Stars Inn, the very essentials of village life. The church has an interesting Perpendicular tower, topped out with an unusual saddleback roof, whilst the inn has earned quite a reputation for its food. The opening of the Winsley Bypass has fortunately removed the incessant stream of lorries and cars from the centre of Winsley, which makes walking these old streets a far more pleasant experience than a few years ago.

3. Keep ahead beyond this stone stile, following an enclosed path for 400 yards downhill to a metal gate and a track on the hilltop above the hamlet of Avoncliff. Turn right, and follow this track downhill for 600 yards to the Kennet and Avon Canal. Cross the canal bridge, and turn immediately right before following the towpath for close on 1½ miles back to Winsley Hill Bridge. About 100 yards before the bridge, a gate on the left gives access to the Fordside Tea Gardens. To complete the walk, pass under Winsley Hill Bridge before crossing the stile on the left to rejoin the B3108 by the parking space.

The Kennet and Avon Canal below Winsley contains no dramatic canal architecture — no locks or aqueducts, wharves or commercial moorings. Rather, it is a tranquil backwater overshadowed by dense tree cover and steep hillsides. One local guidebook uses adjectives such as 'sylvan' and 'resplendent' to describe this section of the canal, adding that 'picturesque' and 'scenic' would appear wholly inadequate appendages!

A tranquil backwater of the Kennet and Avon Canal

Walk 12
GEORGIAN BATH

*W*ith its quite exceptional Georgian architecture — as well as the famous Roman Baths — it comes as little surprise to discover that Bath carries the accolade of being a World Heritage City. Throughout the centuries, the rich and famous — including William Pitt, Thomas Gainsborough and Jane Austen — have made the city their second home. As well as the historic abbey and the Georgian delights of Great Pulteney Street, this walk explores both the Kennet and Avon Canal and the River Avon as these waterways carve a course through the heart of this historic city. This is altogether the most perfect of town trails.

Hidden away in one of the many side streets and alleyways that surround Bath Abbey is Sally Lunn's House. Dating from 1482, this is the oldest house in the whole of the city. Now a truly exquisite tearoom, Sally Lunn's sits firmly on the tourist trail, a 'must-see' attraction for visitors to Bath from Japan, North America and other far-flung parts of the globe. The world-famous Bath Bun, for example, is still baked on the premises to Sally Lunn's original 1680 recipe. It is, as the guidebooks point out, a perfect meal as well as a mouth-watering sweet treat. There are also cream teas — featuring homemade scones and jam as well as Somerset clotted cream — a delicious selection of cakes, coffees and sandwiches. In the evenings, visitors can also sample the acclaimed and historic English Trencher dinner. If all of this isn't enough to tempt you to visit Sally Lunn's, visitors can also explore a small museum to see where Sally Lunn herself worked in 1680. It is altogether the most English of tearooms. Open from 10 am every day. Telephone: 01225 461634.

DISTANCE: 2½ miles.

MAPS: OS Landranger 172 or Explorer 155.

STARTING POINT: Park on the roadside on Bathwick Hill in Bath, just above the point where the road crosses the Kennet and Avon Canal (GR 758649).

HOW TO GET THERE: Follow the A36 around the eastern fringes of Bath city centre and, at the roundabout 150 yards south of the Holburne Museum, turn onto Bathwick Hill — signposted to the University and the American Museum. In 250 yards, having passed the local Mercedes dealership and crossed the Kennet and Avon Canal, park on the roadside wherever convenient.

THE WALK

1. Immediately above the Mercedes dealership on Bathwick Hill, descend a flight of steps to join the Kennet and Avon Canal towpath. Follow the towpath for ½ mile down to Bath Deep Lock, immediately before the A36 in Widcombe. Cross the footbridge on the bottom set of lock gates, turn right down a flight of steps that pass beneath the A36 and continue following the canal down to Thimble Mill and its junction with the River Avon. Immediately before the confluence of these two waterways, cross over bridge 194 and follow the River Avon upstream for ½ mile to Pulteney Bridge and the Horseshoe Falls, passing under a railway bridge and North Parade Bridge along the way. In the shadow of Pulteney Bridge lies the Riverside Café. Just past this café, climb a flight of steps up to Argyle Street and Pulteney Bridge.

Pulteney Bridge was erected in 1770, based upon designs by Robert Adam. Its construction provided an elegant thoroughfare from the centre of the city, across the River Avon to Great Pulteney Street — arguably the finest Georgian terrace in Britain — and on to the elegant Sydney Hotel set in its glorious pleasure

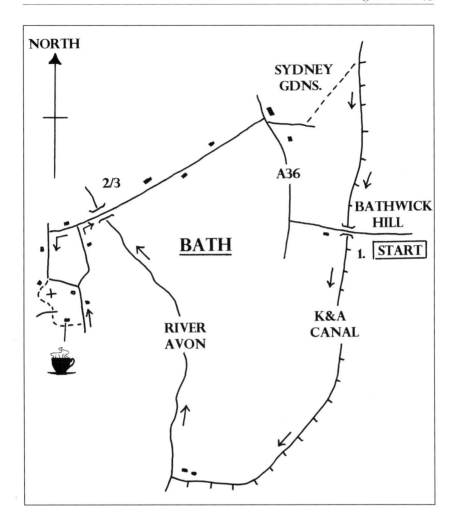

gardens. *Today, the Sydney Hotel is the Holburne Museum and its grounds are the Sydney Gardens public park. Pulteney Bridge is one of the most distinct landmarks in the city, and is the only bridge in Britain to be lined with shops. Customers visiting these business premises can gaze down onto the river below, and the splendid curves of the Horseshoe Falls.*

2. Turn left, cross Pulteney Bridge and continue ahead along Bridge Street. Having passed the Victoria Art Gallery on the left-hand side, carry straight on until you reach the High Street. Turn left, and head down to the clearly visible Bath Abbey. Follow the abbey to the right into the

Abbey Courtyard, turn left to pass in front of the entrance to the abbey before continuing across the Abbey Courtyard — the Roman Baths to the right — to reach York Street. Cross York Street, and follow Church Street down to Abbey Green, before turning left along North Parade Passage. Partway along North Parade Passage, you will pass Sally Lunn's on the left. Continue out to Orange Grove — known colloquially as Bog Island — before heading to the left towards the imposing Empire Hotel. Just by the Empire Hotel, turn right to cross the main road before heading to the left along Grand Parade to return to Pulteney Bridge, the River Avon down below on the right.

Bath Abbey, a late 15th-century ecclesiastical building, was constructed on the site of a Saxon and Norman abbey. It is a fine example of the Perpendicular period of English Gothic architecture. Its many notable features include the fine tower, the west façade portraying the ladder dream of Bishop Oliver King, the heavily carved west door set in a triple arch and the enormous clerestory windows. The courtyard bordering the main entrance to the abbey is one of the liveliest spots in Bath, being a favourite busking location for local entertainers.

The River Avon at Bath

3. Turn right across Pulteney Bridge, and walk the whole length of Great Pulteney Street to the A36 and to the Holburne Museum. Cross the A36, and follow Sydney Place alongside the museum. In 100 yards, turn left through an archway into Sydney Gardens. Head across to the pillared stone shelter, turn right over the railway line and continue following the path up through the park. Immediately before the canal bridge, turn right along a side path for a few yards before turning left through a gateway to join the K&A towpath. Turn right, and follow the canal through an ornate tunnel. At the far end of this tunnel, cross the canal by means of a footbridge adjoining Cleveland House before continuing along the towpath for a further ¼ mile. Keep on the path at this point as it slopes uphill to join Bathwick Hill, just above the Mercedes dealership.

The Kennet and Avon Canal was granted Royal Assent in 1794 and work on this waterway that provided a direct link between Bristol and London was completed 16 years later. The Bath Herald was able to report that 'the guns were fired on Sydney Wharf' alongside the canal's headquarters in Cleveland House. As the canal passes through Sydney Gardens, visitors marvel at the intricate iron footbridges that cross the waterway, as well as the Sydney Gardens tunnel whose entrances are formed of ornately carved and decorated Bath stone. The city's burghers were so concerned at the arrival of the waterway in Bath that they insisted on a style of architecture that would blend in with their fine city.

Walk 13
CLEVEDON and the BRISTOL CHANNEL

The Bristol Channel resort of Clevedon is the nearest genuine seaside resort to either Bath or Bristol. For many older Bristolians, a day-trip to Clevedon, with its grand Victorian residences and its much-loved pier, was their first taste of the sea. This fine coastal excursion sets off along Clevedon's promenade to Wain's Hill, a headland that overlooks the Bristol Channel. The footpath around the headland is known locally as 'Poet's Walk' on account of its association with the poet Coleridge, who once lived in a nearby cottage on Old Church Road, and various other literary figures. It certainly is a most inspiring spot, with its far-ranging vistas across the channel towards the Welsh Hills.

Clevedon is a rather sedate Victorian seaside resort that sits proudly above the Bristol Channel. At the northern end of the promenade, opposite the entrance to Clevedon Pier, stands Scarlett's, a seafront café and tearoom. On cold windy days, customers can shelter indoors and enjoy refreshments, whilst on sunny days, tables and chairs on the front patio will ensure fine views across the Bristol Channel to the Welsh coast. Scarlett's offers morning coffee and afternoon teas, as well as snacks and meals at lunchtime. There is also a rather tempting choice of cooked breakfasts! A wide range of cakes is available, including caramel shortbread, carrot cake, bread and butter pudding and toasted teacakes, as well as the option of a traditional English cream tea. An interesting selection of ice creams from the Marshfield Dairy near Bath is also available, as well as soups such as carrot & coriander, wild mushroom and leek & potato. Open during normal business hours, seven days a week. Telephone: 01275 349032.

DISTANCE: 2½ miles.

MAPS: OS Landranger 172 or Explorer 153.

STARTING POINT: The seafront at Clevedon. Park as close as possible to the pier (GR 402719).

HOW TO GET THERE: Leave the M5 motorway at junction 20, and follow the signs for Clevedon. At the first roundabout, take the left turn signposted to the seafront. Continue following the signs to the seafront, where you will find free parking on the promenade just below the pier.

THE WALK

1. Walk along Clevedon's promenade away from the pier, passing along the way Clevedon Sailing Club, the local bandstand and the Little Harp Inn before reaching — at the southern end of the promenade — a hostelry called the Salthouse. Climb the steps to the right of the Salthouse — the Poet's Walk — that ascend through woodland before reaching the open ground atop Church Hill. Cross to the far side of the hilltop — the churchyard below on the right — before dropping down to join a tarmac path. Follow this to the right, down to the entrance to St Andrew's church.

The 'Poet's Walk' is named after Clevedon's association with such literary figures as the novelist William Thackeray, and the poets Samuel Taylor Coleridge and Lord Tennyson. Tennyson's closest friend at Cambridge had been Arthur Hallam, nephew of Sir Charles Elton of Clevedon Court. Tennyson's well-known poem 'In Memoriam' was written in the year that he visited Hallam's tomb in Clevedon. It is a poem full of classic quotations, perhaps the most noted being:

Tis better to have loved and lost,
Than never to have loved at all.

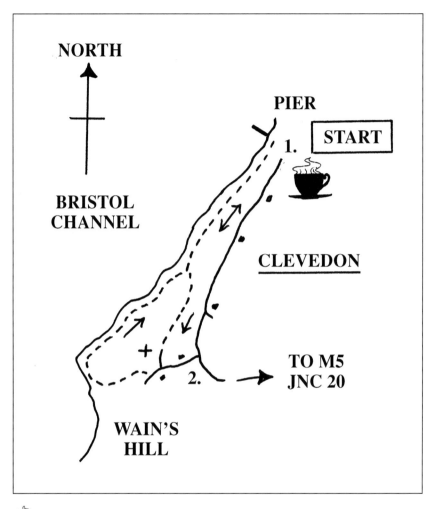

🍵 **2.** Follow the access drive ahead towards the cemetery, and down to its junction with Old Church Road. Turn right, and follow Old Church Road to a point where it meets a wooden barrier before entering a boatyard. Beyond this barrier, follow the tarmac path to the right onto Wain's Hill. Continue on this tarmac path around the perimeter of this rocky promontory until it drops down to the edge of the Marine Lake at the southern end of Clevedon's promenade. Follow the path as it bears right, back to the foot of the steps climbed onto Church Hill at the outset. Turn left, and retrace your steps along the promenade, back to the pier, where Scarlett's awaits you.

Clevedon pier

Clevedon Pier, the town's most famous Victorian landmark, was constructed in 1869 of iron rails originally intended for use on Brunel's South Wales Railway. Part of the pier collapsed during a safety check in October 1970, leaving the pavilion standing forlornly at sea. Appeals were launched for its restoration, with support coming from such famous luminaries as Sir John Betjeman: 'It recalls a painting by Turner, or an etching by Whistler or Sickert, or even a Japanese print.... Without its pier, Clevedon would be a diamond with a flaw.' A Pier Trust was formed and with major financial contributions from the Historic Buildings Council and the National Heritage Memorial Fund, structural repairs to the pier were completed. The pier is now once again open to the public, a monument to Clevedon's Victorian heritage.

Walk 14
CHEW VALLEY LAKE and CHEW MAGNA

A vast reservoir that supplies much of Bristol's water, a riverside path, a village of great antiquity and views across the North Somerset countryside toward the Mendip Hills all combine to make this a most rewarding walk in the heart of the Chew Valley. Although the flanks of Knowle Hill are crossed along the way, the gradients throughout are gentle and well within the capabilities of even the most occasional of walkers. The prospect of refreshments in a spot overlooking the waters of Chew Valley Lake will surely act as a spur should spirits flag along the way!

The Chew Valley Lake Tea Shop really does enjoy a most idyllic location, perched in a slightly elevated position immediately above Chew Valley reservoir. Visitors can relax and enjoy an outlook across the lake towards the Mendip Hills. Scattered around the water's edge are the local fly fishermen, trying to lure the rainbow trout for which Chew is so famous, whilst on the water itself are the yachts and other small craft belonging to the local sailing club. Inside the relatively modern tearoom are a good number of comfortable table and chair sets, with picture windows looking out over the water. It is quite the perfect place to enjoy the varied menu that, in addition to cream teas, coffees and soft drinks, also includes sandwiches, toasties and baguettes. There is also a tempting array of cakes that might include lemon shortbread, flapjacks, doughnuts and iced buns. On a fine day, the traditional English cuppa can be enjoyed on one of the two attractively landscaped picnic areas in front of the teashop. Open every day from 10.30 am, to 5.30 pm in summer and to 4.30 pm in winter. Telephone: 01275 333345.

DISTANCE: 3½ miles.

MAPS: OS Landranger 172 or Explorer 155.

STARTING POINT: The picnic area that houses the Chew Valley Lake Tea Shop, at the northern end of Chew Valley Lake (GR 573614).

HOW TO GET THERE: Follow the A368 road, which links Bath and Weston-super-Mare, to the village of Bishop Sutton. At the eastern end of the village, turn onto the unclassified road that is signposted to Chew Valley Lake. In just over 1 mile, this road passes a picnic area on the left. Continue along the road for another ½ mile before turning off into the next picnic area. There is plenty of parking (fee payable) in the large car park alongside Chew Valley Lake and the Chew Valley Lake Tea Shop.

THE WALK

1. Join the road behind the tearoom, turn left and walk the short distance to a junction with Denny Lane. Immediately past this junction, cross a stile on the right and follow a path through some trees into a field. Continue ahead along the right edge of this field to reach an access road leading to a Bristol Waterworks installation. Turn left, and follow this road downhill. In the valley bottom, just before a bridge that crosses the Chew, turn right along a signposted path into an area of woodland. Follow the woodland path to a stile, before continuing through another area of woodland to a second stile and open fields. Head directly across the next five fields, following the River Chew downstream for close on 1 mile, with stiles marking the course of the right-of-way. The river meanders across meadows, whilst the right-of-way takes a more direct route to the right of the water's edge.

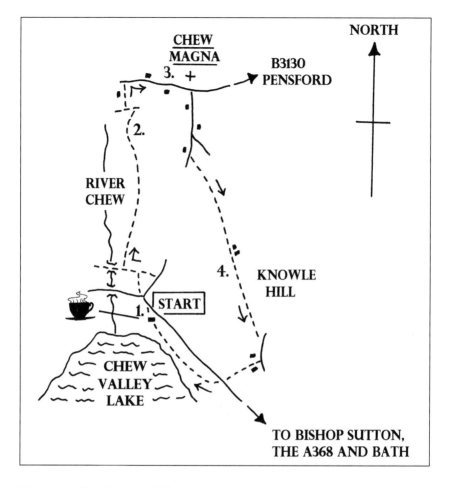

The River Chew has an idyllic source with its headwaters rising magnificently from a rock face behind a row of neat cottages in Chewton Mendip. The Chew then flows in a north-westerly direction through to Chew Magna, before making a 90° turn to flow through Stanton Drew and Pensford to reach the Bristol Avon at Keynsham. Despite being less than 20 miles in length, the Chew has played a significant part in the lives of local people over many hundreds of years. Waterborne rafts brought stone to Stanton Drew for the construction of a Bronze Age stone circle, whilst many hundreds of years later the river powered fulling mills up and down its length. Today, the river is best known for being the source of the water supply for both the Litton Reservoirs and Chew Valley Lake. In so doing, the citizens of Bristol owe this diminutive watercourse a notable debt.

2. In the far left corner of the fifth field, cross a stile and follow a short section of enclosed path to the right to a junction. Turn left, and follow a bridleway across a stream and onto a bridge over the River Chew. Cross the river, turn right and follow a path up to the B3130 in Chew Magna. Turn right, and follow the raised pavement into the centre of the village.

Described as a 'pretty clothing town' by Leland, Henry VIII's antiquary, Chew Magna's prosperity was founded upon cloth, stockings, edge tools and ruddle, a substance used to mark sheep. The grand houses that line the main street are testament to Chew Magna's former prosperity, which has continued to this day with the village lying at the heart of what is colloquially known as 'Bristol's stockbroker belt'. The village is centred upon St Andrew's church, whose origins can be traced back to Norman times. Local guidebooks point visitors towards the preaching cross in the churchyard, as well as the Church House. It was in this early 16th-century building that the churchwardens at one time brewed fine ales for festive occasions.

3. Immediately past the Pelican Inn, turn right into Tunbridge Road, signposted to Bishop Sutton and Bath. In 600 yards, turn right into Denny Lane. Follow this lane for 150 yards before turning left along an enclosed path shown on the OS sheets as 'Pitts Lane'. Follow this footpath for ½ mile until it enters an open field, passing through one handgate along the way. Follow the left edge of this field towards a property. Pass to the right of this property to reach a stile in the end field boundary. Cross this stile and follow the left edge of the field beyond for 100 yards to a gate and a path. Follow this enclosed path up past a property to a handgate and the common land around Knowle Hill.

Despite being less than 400 feet above sea-level, the view from Knowle Hill really is most impressive. The outlook across Chew Valley Lake towards the Mendip Hills above Burrington Combe will linger long in the memory. Readers fortunate enough to track down a copy of John Haddon's 'Portrait of Avon' will discover an aerial view of this quiet corner of North Somerset taken by 'West Air Photography' and some shot it is too! Knowle Hill, incidentally, lies on the little known 'Three Peaks Trail'. This 17-mile circular walk, which also takes in Maes Hill and Blackberry Hill, connects the villages of Pensford, Clutton and Chew Magna. Details of the walk can be obtained from Bath & North East Somerset Council's Development and Environmental Services Department in Bath.

4. Keep directly ahead along the right edge of the common, Knowle Hill an almost obligatory detour on the left-hand side. Keep on the path as it enters the woodland bordering the common, before descending to join a lane by Knowle Hill Farm. Turn right, pass in front of Knowle House and then turn right across a cattle grid to follow a signposted path that runs along a gravelled driveway in front of a property called the Old Granary. Immediately past this property, cross a gate on the left before turning right to follow the edges of two fields down to a stile and the road running from Bishop Sutton to Chew Magna. Turn right and, in a short distance, left into a picnic area by Chew Valley Lake. Pass through a copse to reach the car park before turning right. Follow the path across a grassy picnic area, and continue along what becomes an enclosed course running alongside the lake itself. Follow this path for close on ½ mile back to the car park by the Chew Valley Lake Tea Shop.

Chew Valley Lake was constructed as a reservoir in the 1950s

Chew Valley Lake's vital statistics make for impressive reading: 2½ miles in length, this vast reservoir has a capacity of some 4,500 million gallons. In the 1950s, a 500 yard long dam was constructed across the River Chew and the slow process of flooding the Chew Valley began. Underwater went the site of a medieval village, an old mill, a Roman villa and countless acres of rich agricultural land. Fortunately, these ancient sites were excavated prior to flooding and various artefacts were removed to the Bristol Museum. The Queen officially opened the reservoir in 1956, since when it has become a haven for ornithologists, fly fishermen, sailors and walkers.

Walk 15
BURRINGTON COMBE and BEACON BATCH

In Southern Britain, Burrington Combe is second only to Cheddar for its spectacular inland cliff scenery. It was here that the Reverend Augustus Toplady took shelter from a storm and was inspired to pen the hymn 'Rock of Ages'. Above Burrington lie the open hilltops of high Mendip, rising to over 1,000 feet above sea-level at Beacon Batch. The views are not surprisingly pretty spectacular, extending across the Bristol Channel to the Welsh Hills and beyond. This is one walk where a clear fine day is more or less obligatory.

 The Burrington Inn is very much a hybrid of restaurant, bar and teashop. Sitting beneath the wooded slopes of Burrington Combe, it may not be an *olde worlde* tearoom, but it will provide welcome rest and refreshment after an exhilarating walk to Beacon Batch, the literal high spot of all Mendip. Morning coffee or afternoon tea can be accompanied by a selection of cakes and pastries that includes scones, custard slices, shortbread, doughnuts and gateaux. The full lunchtime menu includes soup, pasties, grills, fish dishes and salads. As well as the main dining area, there is also a conservatory and a number of outdoor picnic tables, which will in all probability be the focus for walkers on a warm summer's day. Open during normal business hours, seven days a week. Telephone: 01761 462227.

DISTANCE: 3½ miles.

MAPS: OS Landranger 182 or Explorer 141.

STARTING POINT: The public car park opposite the Rock of Ages in Burrington Combe, just above the Burrington Inn (GR 477588).

HOW TO GET THERE: Burrington Combe lies just south of the A368, which links Bath and Weston-super-Mare, 10 miles from Weston. Leave the A368 at Burrington to follow the B3134 for just ½ mile into Burrington Combe. The Burrington Inn and the parking area lie alongside the road.

THE WALK

1. Cross the B3134 to the Rock of Ages, before following the footpath through the woodland that runs parallel to the road. In 250 yards, keep on this path as it bears right up and away from the road to follow the rocky — occasionally wet — bed of West Twin Brook. Continue following this rocky valley for 150 yards to a spring on the right bounded by a concrete enclosure. Immediately past the spring, bear right to follow a steep path uphill onto open hillside. In 75 yards, at a junction of paths, turn right and, in another 100 yards, at the next junction, turn left. Follow the clearly visible path uphill, West Twin Brook in the dip away on the left-hand side. Continue on uphill for ½ mile to a prominent crosstrack high on Blackdown, ignoring any side turnings along the way. You are now close on 1,000 feet above sea-level.

Opposite the car park is the famous 'Rock of Ages', a huge vertical limestone cliff inlaid with a substantial crack or cleft. An inscription on the rock reads:

ROCK OF AGES
This rock derives its name
From the well-known hymn written about 1762
By the Rev. A.M. Toplady
Who was inspired whilst sheltering in this cleft during a storm.

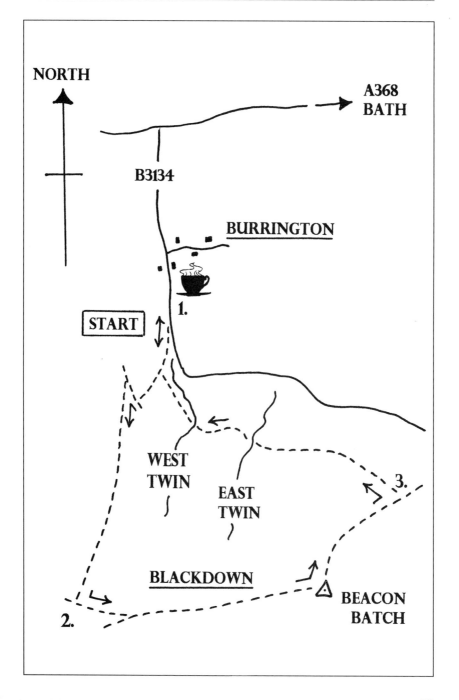

The Rock of Ages

Toplady was a curate at nearby Blagdon and was returning home on horseback when a thunderstorm struck. Having viewed the source of their inspiration, those immortal words 'Rock of ages cleft for me, Let me hide myself in Thee' will now take on a whole new imagery.

2. Turn left, and follow the hilltop path for 250 yards to a point where a path comes in from the right. Follow this path ahead for 600 yards to reach the trig point on Beacon Batch standing at 1,068 feet above sea-level. Follow the path to the left of the trig point downhill towards the distant Ellick House. In ½ mile, almost at the foot of the slope, turn left along a bridleway carrying a 'Limestone Link' sign, with a hedgerow and open field on the right.

Beacon Batch is the highest point on Mendip. From the trig point, the views are immense and almost defy description. The Bristol Channel, the Welsh Hills, Chew and Blagdon Reservoirs, Exmoor... the landmarks are many. It is worth taking the OS Landranger sheet on this walk to try and identify the towns, villages and other such landmarks so clearly visible from this lofty hilltop.

3. Follow this path along the foot of Blackdown, the hedgerow on the right, for just over ½ mile until the path drops down to cross East Twin Brook. Beyond this stream, continue on the path across the hillside for 350 yards until it descends to cross West Twin Brook. Climb the slope beyond this stream and, in a short distance, fork right onto an ill-defined path that drops downhill into the wooded valley containing the aforementioned West Twin Brook. Drop down to the concrete enclosure housing a spring, passed earlier, before following the stream bed back down to the B3134. Turn left, and retrace your steps back to Burrington Combe and the Burrington Inn, passing the entrance to Aveline's Hole along the way.

Aveline's Hole, one of the many potholes and caves to be found on the Mendip Hills, is the result of acidic rainwater reacting with the local limestone. Whilst rabbit-hunting in 1797, two men discovered this cave together with its contents — 50 human skeletons! It was an ancient Stone Age burial chamber.

Walk 16
CHEDDAR and the GORGE

This walk follows the paths atop the cliffs on both sides of Cheddar Gorge, high above the road and looking down on the tourist traffic below. From Black Rock, there is a short steep climb to gain height, before a steady descent down the eastern side of the Gorge into Cheddar. The path is unfenced, and the drop over the cliff-edge several hundred feet so particular care needs to be taken on this stretch. The return to Black Rock along the western side of the Gorge starts with a mile of strenuous uphill walking, before level paths and glorious views are obtained, but you can refresh yourself at a delightful tearoom in Cheddar, and the stunning clifftop scenery will more than repay your efforts!

 From beneath the south-facing slopes of the Mendip Hills, a subterranean stream emerges and flows down through the heart of Cheddar. This stream, which joins the River Axe a mile or two downstream, forms an attractive pool in the centre of the village, set against a backdrop of the most spectacular inland cliff scenery in southern Britain. On the hillside just above this water feature lies the Hillside Cottage tearoom, a charming stone property where you will be able to rest awhile and take refreshment at the halfway point on this walk. In addition to pots of tea and steaming mugs of coffee, Hillside Cottage also offers its customers cream teas, soft drinks, flapjacks, cherry shortbread, scones and a whole host of other goodies. For lunch, light snacks are available, including sandwiches and pasties. The teashop also houses a gift shop where postcards and other souvenirs of your visit to Cheddar can be purchased. It is altogether a quite perfect spot to linger, especially at one of the outside tables with their views of the village and the surrounding cliff scenery. Open every day: 10.30 am to 5.30 pm from Easter to the end of October and 11 am to 5 pm during the winter months. Telephone: 01934 743158.

DISTANCE: 4 miles.

MAPS: OS Landranger 182 or Explorer 141.

STARTING POINT: The rough parking area at the head of Cheddar Gorge by the entrance to the Blackrock Reserve (GR 482545).

HOW TO GET THERE: Blackrock Gate lies 1½ miles from Cheddar on the B3135 road to Chewton Mendip.

THE WALK

1. From the entrance to the Blackrock Reserve, cross the B3135 to the stile opposite, before following a steep rocky path uphill. In 250 yards, on the hilltop, the path reaches a wooden gate and a West Mendip Way marker post. Follow the path ahead through scrubland to a point where the path forks. Ignore the left fork to Draycott, keeping ahead instead on the Cheddar Showcaves Gorge Walk. In 250 yards, cross a stile and continue along the path — a fence on the left — until you emerge onto the open hilltops above the Gorge. Follow the path across the hilltop and on downhill into Cheddar, reaching an observation tower in 1 mile. Immediately before this tower, turn right and head downhill on a flight of steps known as Jacob's Ladder. At the foot of these steps, you will emerge onto the main road in Cheddar.

The Gorge is one of the most famous natural features in the British Isles. It was carved out of the limestone by rivers that now pass deep underground, leaving vertical cliffs of up to 450 feet in height. The path from Black Rock to Cheddar passes literally along the top of these cliffs, and brings what must be one of the most dramatic views in the South of England. In the foreground is Cheddar and the Gorge, whilst beyond lie the Somerset Levels, Glastonbury Tor, Brent Knoll,

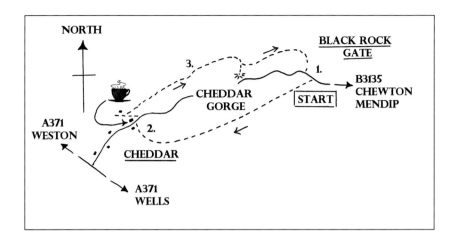

Bridgwater Bay and the Quantock Hills. In Cheddar itself, there are a number of commercially operated caves that are open to the public all year round. Visitors to Gough's Cave and Cox's Cave can marvel at the quite exceptional stalactite and stalagmite formations.

☕ **2.** Turn right and follow the road for 150 yards, passing a pool on the left above which lies the Hillside Cottage tearoom. Just above this pool, turn left in front of Rose Cottage. Pass to the right of a whitewashed cottage, and follow the footpath — initially an unmetalled road — beyond some gateposts. Keep on this track — it soon becomes a metalled drive leading to a property. On reaching the private entrance to this property in 150 yards, turn sharp right and follow an enclosed footpath around the side of the property itself. Continue along this path as far as a second house, before turning sharp right along the footpath that leads steeply uphill. In ¼ mile, pass through a gate in a stone wall, and continue on uphill for another ¼ mile to a stile by a wall.

3. Cross this stile, continue ahead for a few paces and then turn right to follow a boundary wall that runs along the side of a rough pasture. In 200 yards, immediately before a short, sharp ascent, turn right through a gap in the wall — there is a Cheddar Showcaves Cliff Walk sign. Almost immediately, at a fork, keep right and continue for 150 yards to a junction and a marker post. At this point, it is worth making a detour — cross the stile opposite and drop down to a viewpoint high above Cheddar Gorge. For the main walk, turn left and head up to the top right corner of the enclosure. Beyond a gateway, continue along a path

— fence on the left — for ½ mile until the path drops down some rough steps. At the bottom of these steps, turn right to reach a gate. Beyond this gate, follow a track down to the B3135 before turning left to return to the parking area at Blackrock Gate.

The climb back up to Black Rock from Cheddar along the western side of the Gorge passes through the National Trust's Cheddar Cliffs property. Once sufficient height has been secured — and aching leg muscles overcome! — the precariousness of the route taken earlier down into Cheddar becomes obvious as remote figures walking the path high on the clifftops on the opposite side of the Gorge come into view. To quote S.P.B. Mais from over 50 years ago: 'The incline became steeper, the winding more intense. The boulders suddenly became high, vertical precipices of limestone, with tall trees growing out of them. Then it became even grander, and more awe-inspiring. In the high gale I felt certain that the rocks were going to fall on me. The cliffs assumed shapes — a lion here, a monkey there.' The passage of time has done little to diminish what must surely rank as one of the ten wonders of the British Isles.

Cheddar Gorge seen from the top of the cliffs

79

Walk 17
WELLS and DINDER

Wells, dominated by its magnificent cathedral, holds the claim of being England's smallest city. Alongside the cathedral stands the moated Bishop's Palace and the Market Place, so much history and tradition that it may well prove difficult to head out into the surrounding countryside! Leave we must, however, as the walk heads eastwards to the neighbouring village of Dinder. This is East Mendip, where King's Castle Wood and Tor Hill dominate the landscape. There are one or two climbs along the way, but nothing too taxing — altogether a pleasant rural excursion in the heart of Somerset.

 Carrington's Tea Room stands on Sadler Street in Wells, a bustling thoroughfare at the western edge of the Cathedral Green. Sadly, there are no views of the magnificent west front of the cathedral, but this will cease to be of concern once the delights of the local cuisine appear on your table. Whether it be a hearty breakfast, a light snack, morning coffee or afternoon tea, there is certain to be something of interest on the menu! In particular, the cream tea is highly recommended. Consisting of a pot of tea, scones, strawberry jam and genuine clotted cream from Somerset, this is just what is needed to restore all of those calories expended whilst crossing a small corner of East Mendip. Instead — or in addition — perhaps flapjacks or teacakes, shortbread or even pavlova will appeal. Open during normal business hours, seven days a week. Telephone: 01749 676435.

DISTANCE: 4½ miles.
MAPS: OS Landranger 182 or Explorer 141.
STARTING POINT: The Market Place in Wells (GR 550458). Sadler Street, location of Carrington's Tea Room, runs north out of the Market Place.
HOW TO GET THERE: Wells lies on the A39 Bath to Glastonbury road, just 5 miles north of Glastonbury. There are several car parks in the city centre, all of which are clearly signposted. When buying your parking ticket, allow 4 hours for the walk and a visit to the tearoom. Directions from the car parks to the Market Place and the cathedral are clearly displayed.

The walk

With its population of just 10,000, Wells is the smallest city in England. It is also the only city in Somerset. Enjoying a magnificent setting against a backdrop of the Mendip Hills, it owes its origins to a series of freshwater springs sited in what are now the grounds of the Bishop's Palace. In the early 8th century, King Ine of Wessex founded a church near to this water source, whilst by AD 766 King Cynewulf had granted land to 'the minister by the Great Spring which they call Wells'. By the 10th century, the diocese of Wells was created, and St Andrew's church became its cathedral. Today's visitors gaze with awe at the splendid west front of the cathedral, as well as the other fine ecclesiastical architecture that includes the Bishops's Palace, Vicar's Close and the lofty 15th century tower on nearby St Cuthbert's church.

1. Pass through the archway — the Bishop's Eye — at the eastern end of the Market Place to follow the path signposted to the Bishop's Palace. Once through the arch, turn right to follow the moat around the Bishop's Palace to the right, the water on your left. At the next corner of the moat, where the water bears left, keep directly ahead past Islington Cottage to a gate and an open field. Pass through a kissing gate to follow a footpath signposted to Dulcote. This is a tarmac path. Follow this path across three fields to reach a kissing gate in the far right corner of the third field. Drop down some steps to join a track, before turning left to walk up to the B3139. Cross to the pavement opposite, turn right and in just 10 yards pass through a wooden kissing gate in the hedgerow on the left.

2. Enter a field, and head straight across to a gate/stile opposite. In the next field, follow the bottom right-hand edge to the far right corner where a gate/stile brings the path to a track. Cross this track to the gate opposite and, in the next field, head across past an isolated oak tree to reach a stile in the opposite hedgerow. In the next field, follow the hedge on the right until, partway across the field — immediately beyond a 'widening' — a handgate appears in the hedge and a sign to Dinder. Pass through the handgate, turn left and follow the hedge on the left to a gate/stile in the left corner of the field. In the next field, head directly ahead to a metal gate in the opposite field boundary and, in one final field — the village cricket pitch — cross to a stile opposite and join the lane in Dinder. Follow this lane to a junction by the village church.

Dinder is a diminutive village lying beneath the south-facing slopes of the Eastern Mendips. Being in the heart of rural Somerset, this is clearly an agriculturally based community, as is evident by such landmarks as Crapnell Farm, whose 300 acres are centred upon a listed 16th-century farmhouse. The guidebooks make few references to the village, other than one which pointed out an ancient Mendip worm in Dinder's medieval church. A rather friendly-looking carving, with a head at each end, it was found in the chancel wall during restoration work in the 19th century. The creature, which dates from a very much earlier chapel that stood on the site, now rests above the rector's stall.

3. Turn left, and follow this lane up out of Dinder until you reach the entrance lodge to Sharcombe Grange. Continue along the lane beyond this lodge for 200 yards to a junction. Turn left, and follow an unsigned bridleway. Follow this track uphill for 200 yards until it enters an open field surrounded by woodland. Cross to the far left corner

The magnificent west front of Wells Cathedral

of this field, pass through a gateway and enter some woodland. Follow the woodland path for 200 yards to a junction on the edge of the woodland — with a golf course beyond — turn right and head uphill for 100 yards to a handgate. Beyond this handgate, turn left to follow a track that runs between the golf course and King's Castle Wood. Follow this track for ½ mile until you reach a large detached stone property on the right.

King's Castle Wood is owned by the Somerset Trust for Nature Conservation. The name appears to refer to an Iron Age hillfort, faint traces of which lie hidden deep within the woodland. The walk passes along the south-facing fringe of the woodland, an excellent spot for butterflies. Gatekeepers and speckled woods may be seen flitting along the hedgerows in high summer, feeding in particular on bramble flowers.

4. Follow the track past this property and cross a stile on the right into a field. Head across to the far right corner of the field where the field narrows to form a grassy path, which bears right and then left around the perimeter of Torhill Quarry. Once past the left turn, continue following

83

the hedge on the left that borders the former quarry to reach a gate/stile at the far end of the field and a National Trust Tor Hill sign. Enter some woodland, and keep ahead for a short distance to a junction. Turn right, and walk through the trees to reach an open field. Cross to the far-left corner of the field, and follow a woodland path downhill to reach a stone slab stile and Torhill Lane. Turn left to reach the B3139, turn right for a short distance before turning left at a gateway to join a path that soon runs alongside the moat around the Bishop's Palace. Follow the moat all of the way around to the archway — the Bishop's Eye — and the Market Place. At the end of the Market Place, turn right into Sadler Street and Carrington's Tea Room is just a short distance along on the right.

Walk 18
SHAPWICK HEATH

The Somerset Levels, a vast area of low-lying former marshland, presents one of the rarest habitats in Britain. This excessively horizontal landscape, which lies mainly below the 30 foot contour line, has to be continuously drained in order to prevent persistent and widespread flooding. Shapwick Heath, a National Nature Reserve, contains the most extensive examples of the various vegetation types in the area, which range from poor fen to bog myrtle pastures to birch and alder woodland. This walk follows the gravelled trackbed of the former Glastonbury Branch Railway across the heart of Shapwick Heath. Although essentially a linear walk, there are several diversions which enable visitors to view the wildfowl of this major wetland from the seclusion of well-positioned hides. What you might spot clearly depends upon the time of year, although little grebe, grey heron, buzzard, kestrel, barn owl and lesser spotted woodpecker are just a few of the species found on Shapwick Heath all year around.

☕ Just to the south of Westhay, what appears to be a fairly standard garden centre is in fact also home to both the Peat Moors Visitors' Centre and the Willows Tea Rooms. Located at one end of the garden centre, the tearoom blends in quite nicely with the surrounding retail displays that, in addition to plants and shrubs, include local crafts, artwork and an RSPB presentation. Outside on the patio, visitors can enjoy their refreshments in the midst of a collection of garden furniture and gnomes! In addition to tea, coffee and soft drinks, the Willows Tea Rooms also offers light lunches and a varied selection of cakes and pastries. The cakes might typically include caramel shortbread, flapjacks, fruit cake, scones and chocolate cake, whilst the lunches encompass salads, soup, sandwiches and eggs on toast. After a delightful stroll across the unique lowland habitat of Shapwick Heath, the Willows is the perfect spot to rest and linger awhile. It is open from 10 am each day. Telephone: 01458 860257. Incidentally, the Railway Inn at Ashcott Corner lies conveniently at the halfway stage on this walk.

DISTANCE: 4½ miles.

MAPS: OS Landranger 182 or Explorer 141.

STARTING POINT: The Willows Garden Centre just north of Shapwick (GR 426415).

HOW TO GET THERE: Follow the B3151 road from Glastonbury to Wedmore as far as Westhay. In the centre of Westhay, head south on the lane signposted to Shapwick. In ¾ mile, the lane passes the Willows Garden Centre.

THE WALK

For many thousands of years, what is now known as the Somerset Levels was an inland sea, covered by water that swept in from Bridgwater Bay and the Bristol Channel. The occasional area of high ground — such as Glastonbury Tor — would quite literally be an island in this sea. As the sea receded, Iron Age tribes built wooden trackways across the marshland, together with lake villages made up of raised roundhouses. Visitors to the Peat Moors Visitors' Centre can see reconstructed roundhouses and trackways. It was during medieval times that rhynes — or drainage ditches — were dug, and it became possible to graze livestock on the Levels. More significantly, the extensive peat deposits became the subject of extraction, initially for domestic fuel and more recently as gardening material. On Shapwick Heath, where peat extraction has ceased, pools and wetlands have once again been developed and the landscape is being restored to create a major new wetland environment. The habitat is home to an interesting butterfly and dragonfly population, whilst roe deer can be seen in the thickets. Mink are also widespread in the reserve.

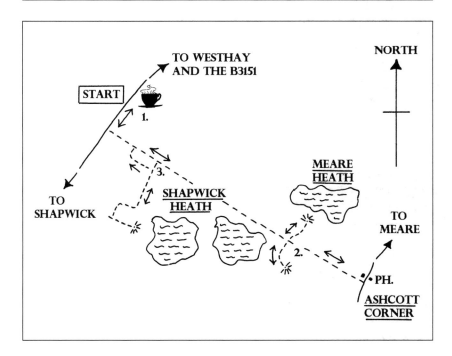

1. Leave the Willows, and turn left along Shapwick Road. In 250 yards, having crossed the South Drain — the waterway that crosses Shapwick Heath — turn left through a gate to enter the Shapwick Heath National Nature Reserve. Follow the gravel track ahead — the former Glastonbury Railway — for close on 2 miles across Shapwick Heath until the path reaches a gate and parking area in Ashcott Corner. Beyond the parking area, if you follow the lane to the left for 100 yards you will find the conveniently placed Railway Inn. To return, go back to the Reserve and start to retrace your steps.

2. Half a mile along the track from Ashcott Corner, you will reach a minor crossroads marked by a footbridge on the right across the South Drain. To find the first hide, turn right over the footbridge and follow the gravelled path through the woodland ahead for 200 yards. This will bring you to the hide overlooking Meare Heath. Alternatively, if you turn left at this crossroads, and follow the footpath to the south for 300 yards, you will find the second hide in this part of the reserve. Having made either or both of these detours, continue along the main track back towards the Willows for 1 mile, the South Drain being your constant companion on the right all the while.

☕ **3.** Look out for a pair of bird boxes attached to poles on the left-hand side followed by the start of a row of telegraph poles. Turn left by the first of the telegraph poles along a gravelled path, before continuing along what becomes a grassy path for 400 yards. Keep on the path at this point as it bears right. In another 200 yards turn left and, in just 100 yards, left again to follow the path out to another hide overlooking the wetlands. Retrace your steps back to the start of that gravelled path, and turn left along a side path. In 150 yards, look out for a section of reconstructed ancient trackway on the right-hand side. Continue along the path — it soon bears right — back up to the main track across Shapwick Heath. Turn left to return to Shapwick Road, where a right turn will return you to the Willows Tea Rooms.

The Peat Moors Visitors' Centre includes a reconstructed roundhouse

Walk 19
GLASTONBURY and the TOR

*G*lastonbury *is widely acknowledged to be one of the most mystical and mysterious places in Britain. The Tor, with its ruinous tower of what was formerly St Michael's church, is but the most visible symbol of the religious mysticism that attracts visitors from far and wide to this otherwise quite normal town. From the heart of Glastonbury, this walk explores the countryside around the Tor, before a final steep ascent to the summit of this most remarkable of landmarks. The views, quite naturally, are outstanding, and range from the Mendip Hills to the north around to the Quantocks and Exmoor. Closer to hand, the outlook extends across the excessively horizontal Somerset Levels towards the Bristol Channel and the Welsh Hills.*

☕ Bear left at the bottom of Glastonbury's High Street and there, opposite the entrance to the abbey, lies the appropriately named Abbey Tea Rooms. With its brightly painted exterior, and bay windows, the attractive teashop proves extremely popular with visitors to the town and its abbey. If you are fortunate enough to secure a window seat, it is quite the perfect place to sit and simply watch the world go by whilst enjoying one of the many enticing options on the menu. You will be somewhat spoiled for choice with selections that include homemade cakes, scones, crumpets, teacakes and shortbread. Many visitors, however, will probably opt for the more than tempting Somerset cream tea, which naturally includes a portion of local clotted cream. If your needs are for something a little more substantial, the Abbey Tea Rooms also offers visitors a choice of light lunches, which typically includes such faithful standbys as beans on toast and toasted sandwiches. Open during normal business hours, seven days a week. Telephone: 01458 832852.

DISTANCE: 4 miles.

MAPS: OS Landranger 182 or Explorer 141.

STARTING POINT: The public car park in Magdalene Street in Glastonbury, at the entrance to the abbey (GR 499388).

HOW TO GET THERE: Glastonbury lies alongside the A39, just a few miles south-west of Wells. On reaching Tin Bridge Roundabout on the northern edge of the town, leave the A39 and follow the road ahead towards the town centre. In just over 1 mile, turn right into the High Street. At the bottom of the High Street, keep left into Magdalene Street where the abbey entrance and car park lie on the left-hand side. If the car park is full, park in one of the other signposted car parks and make your way to the starting point accordingly.

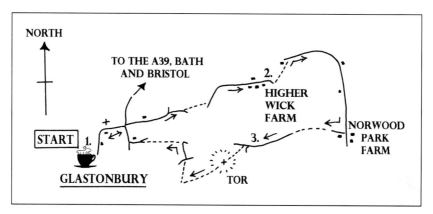

THE WALK

1. Walk to the top of the High Street, and follow the road opposite called Bove Town. In 300 yards, where this road bears left and becomes the Old Wells Road, keep ahead along the quieter lane known as Wick Hollow. In 100 yards, at the top of the climb through the hollow, there is a seat on the left and a footpath that runs parallel to the road. Follow this footpath, walking in the same direction as before, up to a gate and an open field. Follow the left edge of this field to a stile in its corner and a quiet lane. Head along this lane to the left down to Higher Wick Farm, all the while enjoying views across the Levels towards Wells.

Glastonbury, with its location below the famous tor, is one of the most identifiable spots in the whole of Great Britain. The town and its environs abound in legends, legends of Arthur and Guinevere, and Joseph of Arimathea and the Holy Grail. It is little wonder that the town is a principal focus of pilgrimage in the West Country. If time permits, visit both Glastonbury Abbey and the Somerset Rural Life Museum. The abbey, despite being little more than a collection of ruined arches and transepts, still retains a deeply religious atmosphere, with its pleasant lawns being a delightful oasis from the busy high street just a few minutes walk away. The Rural Life Museum, housed in the 14th-century Abbey Barn, chronicles the lives and times of the rural communities in this corner of the county.

2. Pass to the left of the farmhouse, cross a cattle grid and continue past Higher Wick Farm and its associated barns. Beyond these barns, keep on an unmetalled track that bears right before reaching a junction. Turn left, and follow a track for 300 yards down to a bungalow called Greenlands and a lane. Turn right, and follow this lane for ¾ mile until you reach Norwood Park Farm on the left and a rank of cottages on the right. Turn right in front of these cottages, and follow a byway uphill for over ¾ mile to a road junction immediately below the Tor.

Glastonbury Tor has a dominance that belies its mere 520 feet of height. This conical-shaped hill rises from the horizontal local landscape to catch the eye of even the most unobservant traveller. The ruined tower that dominates the hilltop is that of the 14th-century St Michael's church, an earlier satellite monastic settlement on the hilltop having been destroyed by either a landslide or earthquake in 1275. The Tor was the site of the local gibbet. Abbot Richard Whiting, the last Abbot of Glastonbury, met his end here in 1539.

3. Follow the lane ahead for 100 yards to a stile on the left and a path that heads towards the Tor. Climb to the top of the Tor, before following the concrete stepped path down the far side of the Tor towards Glastonbury. At the bottom of the concrete path, pass a stile into the next field. Bear half right across this field to a stile in its far right corner where the path joins a lane. Turn right and, in just 20 yards, left by a bungalow along a side lane. In 150 yards, where the lane bears right, turn left along a path to reach a kissing gate and a hillside field. Head downhill across this field, following a well-worn path, to a gate at the foot of the slope. Continue down a road to reach a junction in a housing development, before continuing down Dod Lane to its junction with Chilkwell Street. Turn right, before taking the second left back into the High Street. Retrace your steps to the car park and the Abbey Tea Rooms.

The mystical Glastonbury Tor

Walk 20
SHEARWATER and LONGBRIDGE DEVERILL

The Longleat Estate is best known for its grand mansion, its safari park and, more recently, the arrival of a Center Parcs leisure complex. Away from the commercial hub of the estate, however, there is a good deal of unspoiled countryside and woodland that offer many opportunities for a few hours peaceful walking in the great outdoors. This walk starts off at Shearwater, an ornamental lake in the south-east corner of the Longleat Estate. From the water's edge, quiet lanes, fieldpaths and tracks are followed in and around the nearby Wylye Valley. A gentle stroll through the delightfully named Foxholes Plantation returns the walk to Shearwater and the Bargates Tearoom.

Shearwater, an ornamental lake in the south-east corner of the Longleat Estate, is a popular destination in the Bath and Bristol area.

Alongside the main entrance to the lake stands a traditional thatched cottage, whose extension houses the Bargates Tearoom. On warm sunny days, most visitors opt to sit outside on the patio or in the gardens at this most idyllic of spots but, rest assured, there is ample seating indoors in the bright and airy tearoom ... which also houses a piano! Teas and coffees, ice creams and soft drinks are available, as well as light lunches. A cream tea might prove an irresistible option, too, as might a slice of flapjack or chocolate cake. Delicious scones and teacakes complete the menu in this off-the-beaten-track tearoom with its delightful rural setting. Open during normal business hours throughout the summer months; the hours are more restricted in the winter — telephone for details: 01985 213255.

DISTANCE: 5 miles.
MAPS: OS Landranger 183 or Explorer 143.
STARTING POINT: Shearwater car park. (GR 853420).
HOW TO GET THERE: Follow the A350 south from the end of the Warminster
    Bypass. In 1½ miles, turn right along the road signposted to Shearwater. Shortly,
    turn left by the Bath Arms and follow the lane for ½ mile to the Shearwater car
    park. The Bargates Tearoom is on the right-hand side just before the car park.

THE WALK

Shearwater is one of the best-known stretches of water in the area. Lying in the south-east of Longleat Estate, this most picturesque lake was constructed way back in 1791 by the Duke of Bridgwater. Rhododendrons grow over the water's edge along most of the shore, whilst the lake itself is surrounded by dense woodland. The plentiful stock of fish, including bream, roach and perch, attract anglers from far and near, whilst ornithologists are drawn to Shearwater by the rich variety of wildfowl that includes grebes, herons and kingfishers, with the surrounding woodland being home to woodpeckers, owls and treecreepers.

1. Leave the car park and turn right, walking along the road by the Bargates Tearoom. In 150 yards, turn left down a lane, which drops down into a valley before climbing to a right-hand bend. About 150 yards past this bend, turn left onto a signposted footpath. Follow this enclosed path uphill into an area of woodland and, ignoring a left turn near the top of the climb, continue on to the Picket Gate to Crockerton Lane. Cross to the stile opposite and walk across a field to a gate opposite. Beyond this gateway, turn right along a signposted bridleway.

2. Follow the enclosed track to a pair of gates, before continuing along the right edges of the next three fields. Almost in the corner of the third

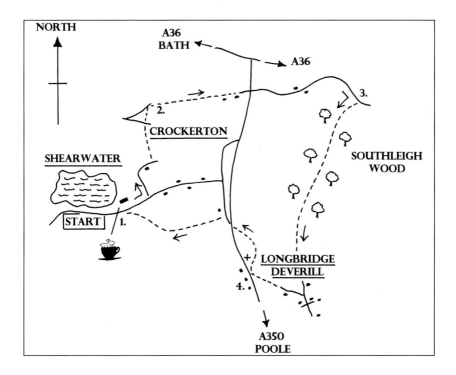

field, pass through a gate, continue along the edge of a garden to a second gate and then follow an enclosed path downhill to a driveway that leads to the A350. Cross over into Five Ash Lane, and follow this lane for ¾ mile. It initially drops down to the River Wylye before climbing uphill into Southleigh Wood. On the hilltop, turn right into the woodland where a bridleway crosses the lane.

Southleigh Wood is largely coniferous woodland, whose rich varieties of trees include larch, grand fir, Norway spruce and western red cedar. The shady woodland paths are quite delightful, and disprove the theory that coniferous woodland is always a bad thing. At the southern end of Southleigh Wood, the path emerges into a hilltop field where a fine view across the Wylye Valley towards Salisbury Plain opens up.

3. Follow the main woodland path due south for ¾ mile, ignoring all left and right turns. At the end of the woodland, pass through a metal gate to enter a hilltop field with glorious views across Wiltshire's downland. Cross to the far right corner of this field, before continuing along a concrete farm road down into Longbridge Deverill. Just before a crossroads, turn right along a back lane by Sand Hill Cottage. In 300 yards, pass through a gateway and bear half left across a field to the River Wylye. Follow the river along to a footbridge, cross the river and continue up towards the A350 before turning right along the lane leading to the village church.

The most characterful part of Longbridge Deverill lies around the early Norman church, where the old school and the Thynne almshouses are also located. The almshouses were founded in 1655 by Sir James Thynne of Longleat, whose family vault lies beneath the north aisle of the church. Another famous Thynne — Sir John — is also buried at Longbridge Deverill. Sir John was the builder of Longleat House. The setting of church and almshouses above the Wylye is most picturesque, despite the incursion of heavy traffic on the A350.

☕ **4.** Enter the churchyard, and pass to the right of the church to reach a kissing gate in the end wall of the churchyard. Cross the next paddock to a gate, before heading half left across the next much larger field. Aim for a stile in the left-hand field boundary, between the third and fourth telegraph poles on the left, before climbing a bank up to the A350. Turn right for a few yards, before following the road opposite signposted to Shearwater. Just past a right-hand bend, turn left along a bridleway into Foxholes Plantation. Follow the track along the southern edge of the woodland, before bearing right along its western edge. Eventually, the path enters the heart of the woodland and bears left to a distinct fork. Bear right at this point, and keep on the main path that shortly bears left and drops downhill back to the car park, with Shearwater and the Bargates Tearoom awaiting you on the other side of the road.

Picturesque Shearwater draws a rich variety of wildlife